BRIAN FABIANO

NEURO MARKET OLOGY

Harness Converging Technologies and Diverging Audiences to Create Dynamic One to One Marketing and Astonishing ROI.

FabCom Publishing
Scottsdale, AZ

www.neuromarketology.com

First published in the United States of America in 2010 by FabCom Publishing.

FabCom Publishing
7819 E. Greenway Rd.
Scottsdale, AZ 85260
Email: info@fabcomlive.com

Typeset by FabCom
Printed and bound in the U.S.A. by FabCom Publishing
Designed by Christen Calhoun

ISBN 978-0-615-37146-7

First Edition

TABLE OF CONTENTS

PREFACE

My purpose in writing this book is to present straightforward, real-world, fact-based guidance on utilizing the converging forces of new and emerging technologies to drive your marketing efforts to hyper-relevance and superior returns. The book is written for those who make the daily decisions in marketing—marketing managers, directors, and vice presidents, and for those who have to live with the results of those decisions—company owners and CEOs.

To get the most out of this book, you may also want to read the work of Trout and Ries, in particular, *Positioning: The Battle for Your Mind* and *The 22 Immutable Laws of Marketing*. Also recommended, *The Long Tail: Why the Future of Business is Selling Less of More*, by Chris Anderson, which redefines the Internet economy. See the bibliography in the back for additional publications that have been foundational building blocks for this book and offer sound, thoughtful advice on marketing and management topics.

Because this book is awash in technology and marketing buzzwords, I have taken a more informal and conversational approach in my writing in order to ensure easier understanding by all readers. As you read, just imagine we're talking about all this over lunch, a very in-depth, eye-opening lunch.

Whenever we use the word product in the book, take it to mean product, service, idea—or, in the largest sense, brand—whatever it is you are trying to promote.

All trademarks referenced in this book are the property of their respective owners.

ACKNOWLEDGMENTS

First of all, I would like to thank the team at FabCom for their tireless work in utilizing new technology and for putting up with my insistence on finding a better way to accomplish the process of marketing. Thank you for building the pathways between the best available to the industry and the idea of what could be. You were determined to find the alternatives to settling for what the industry settles for, what customers settle for, and what manufacturers and software developers settle for.

Only through this kind of constant probing and "what if" questioning were we able to push years ahead of the curve as early adopters. Our team was able to untangle the new capabilities presented by the convergence of technology and migration of the markets themselves to offer our clients true innovation that outperforms the standards created by those before us.

This spirit of innovation and going beyond what others have already accomplished to achieve what needs to be done is at the heart of this book. The resulting dynamic cross-channel marketing methodology created the explosion of our agency's growth and unprecedented return on investment for those that have implemented this new methodology. This culture of seeking a better way has driven all of the progression you will read about within the pages of this book.

Thank you to all the administrators, strategists, copywriters, and creative and art directors who turned their workflows upside down to create a perfect marriage with the programmers, data architects, and software engineers at our company—your deeds have produced a thriving agency in a changing economy, and the insights in this book.

Special thanks to Bob House, our agency's chief copywriter, who helped take years of experience formulating the individual elements that have come to develop this new methodology from within a myriad of industry sectors and helped me organize them logically. I type with five fingers, and I would still be penning this book if not for Bob House and his assistance.

In addition, I want to thank Joe Bardin, the copy maestro who helped me edit the book. After a year of Bob and I working together for completion, he polished the final draft and was able to add clarity for those that would be exposed to this thinking for the first time. He was the key person who helped me see the proverbial forest of understanding through the trees of creation. He added the outside perspective in my effort to detail the steps to capitalize on this new progression of marketing.

I also want to thank my family, the anchor of my life. My two children are the reason for my continual efforts. They have kept me focused on the greater good of others and have helped me stay enthusiastic building the agency and, thus, the methodology and breakthroughs we have discovered in the process.

Finally, I would like to publicly thank my bride of twenty-one years. She is a copywriter by trade and is also an author. I thank her for letting me invade her turf as an author in order to help the industry adopt a new way of thinking about marketing. It is only through her love, support, and constant vigilance in raising our children that I was provided the time and ability to build the agency and this methodology. But her contribution doesn't end there. Her world class editing skills have made this book viable to read. Her ability to work with me as an editor, combined with her understanding of how I think, was invaluable to this effort.

Lastly, but most importantly, thank you to all our customers who have trusted us with their brands, their budgets, and lifeblood over the years. We never would have found the better way if they had not shown faith in our unprecedented strategies. They trusted us in the early days of developing our new approach. That trust provided us the opportunity to take their marketing to another level of effectiveness and prove the model for those to come.

INTRODUCTION

There are moments in the history of our industry in which new conditions and new technology combine to offer evolutions that break through the existing standards and the results of conventional, best practice thinking. Take the facsimile machine or cellular phone, for example. They were evolutions of existing accepted processes and technology. The fax was an extension of copier technology, and the cell phone was an evolution of one-hundred-year-old technology that had not moved forward in years. They both were game changers.

Neuromarketology™ and the resulting new marketing capabilities described in this book are comparable. The fax and the cell phone took a few years to penetrate the mainstream. So will this new hybrid of dynamic integrated, and personally relevant, one to one database marketing. The innovations brought on by the convergence of new and old communication platforms, new protocols, more bandwidth, automated data mining, dynamic analytics, and the explosion of new and emerging consumer communication channels, multiplied by the wave of individualized personal communication devices, are paving the way to extraordinary return on marketing investments. The marketers that know how to utilize the customers' own interactions and typically siloed information in real-time are harnessing the true power of this evolution.

Significant market share goes to the early adopters. Just like the desktop publishing revolution or the advent of the Internet, there will be early adopters, majority adopters, and late adopters. Being an early adopter of this methodology will provide rocket fuel to your marketing efforts just like the Internet did in the last decade. But either way, there is no stopping this breakthrough in communications and marketing. Within a few years this new methodology will be the standard, just as by the year 2000 everyone was getting on the web. Those firms who understood with clarity the changes in the marketing landscape because of the advent of the Internet were clear winners. They grabbed the best URLs; they made swift and efficient gains in market share. Overnight they created brands that eclipsed the brands that had dominated for decades. Small companies ate up the big ones who were slow to adopt.

This book, the thinking and technology, is *your* opportunity to see what is developing and adopt a marketing methodology that has proven to generate a three-to-one return on your investment and consistently superior results over conventional marketing best practices. That's more sales, more loyalty, and a higher return on your marketing investment. This is a value equation that continues to accelerate. Read on and learn how Neuromarketology™ can give your marketing wings.

What is Neuromarketology™?

Neuromarketology™ is the study of reactions driven from the brain based on the exposure to specific marketing messages, imagery, and timing. It's the science of knowing each of your target audience's emotional connection points and the methodology of configuring your marketing messages to connect your brand attributes with each stakeholder in the most relevant manner for that specific target.

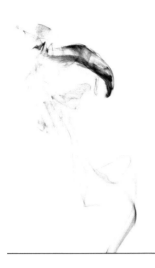

CHAPTER 1

Clarity Out of Chaos

The cross media moment

Marketing today is chaotic, right? Too much noise. Too many channels. Too much guess work and not nearly enough in the way of returns. Traditional strategies are failing to deliver traditional results. And prospects are only getting pickier when it comes to responding to your marketing messages.

But what if the new marketing environment that confounds traditional strategies holds incredible opportunities as well? What if the technology that has scattered audiences, over-saturated them with advertising and made them ultra-selective could be leveraged for superior returns? What if all the chaos could be organized and deployed at your disposal, enabling you to market like the Fortune 100 companies and accomplish the task all naturally within the confines of your existing brand, company, and budgets?

You can. And this book will show you how.

When markets fundamentally alter, when the entire basis for commerce undergoes transformation, the existing truths of conventional wisdom must shift to keep up. Read on as we unwind the implications of numerous, often idiosyncratic changes in our business, that have combined to support a huge paradigm shift for marketers who have the insight to bring it together.

We're witnessing a historic confluence of conditions, technologies, and human excellence, which, though they may have incubated separately, have now boomeranged into a single convergence of capability and opportunity that fundamentally redefines the "one to many" mass marketing model.

Traditional mass marketing brand strategy required that we identify the single group most likely to purchase and then develop the single consistent message that will best move that one group to buy. If you got your strategy right, and your communications and creative were up to it, success equaled a 2 percent return.

A new methodology has emerged that enables you to harness the true power of your brand by mapping to all your appropriate audiences on a true one to one basis, rather than simply the one group most likely to buy. For the cost of fishing in one or two ponds, you can now drop your hook into every relevant pond out there, and catch the best fish in each.

For some, resisting this new methodology is about job security. They spread a covering fog that usually manifests itself in statements or thoughts such as: "been there, done that," "our industry or customers are different," "we don't have time for this nor the staff."

But the fact is, even if we, as marketers, wanted to stand pat, to repeat what worked in the past, we can't; it's over, it's obsolete. These days, that 2 percent response, which has been our gold standard, has grown more and more elusive. Conventional campaigns don't get the job done anymore.

Our audiences are no longer relaxing in front of the TV every Thursday night watching the *Cosby Show* on an NBC network affiliate, the place they congregated when all our modern conventional wisdom was formed.

So, where are they? Everywhere!

The communications marketplace has exploded, splintering audiences into hundreds of different channels across multiple media options. How do you reach deep into the new channels out there? How do you make the most of the social networking tools now available? How do you target and market to these radically divergent audiences?

Clearly, a new paradigm is needed. One that leverages the disparate communication channels and incredible digital power of the Google generation, as well as cracking the limitations of one to one dynamic marketing. While some bemoan the loss of access to mass unified audiences, the leading edge of marketing has moved on.

This book will outline a series of advancements in technology, science, and society some forty years in the making. Some of the advancements have appeared in the last few years, while others are still emerging. The true powers of this evolution have recently linked together in such a way that a new methodology has emerged. This new neuromarketing methodology offers forward-thinking marketers opportunities to lower the barriers to new markets and propel their brands into the new communication channels with sustainable, holistic growth.

Some of the advancements are incremental, like content availability or online adoption; some of them are substantial, such as digital photography and desktop audio and video, but have been taken for granted before marketers harnessed their true power. Some advancements are innocuously morphing before our very eyes, such as bandwidth, dynamic database accessibility, public GPS interactivity, and social networking.

Many of these capabilities are known individually, deployed for their original intent (like content aggregation), and then their practitioners have moved on to the next big flavor, tactic, method, or technology of the month. But the true collective power of these advancing marketing capabilities and new possibilities are fleeting for most marketers—until we link them together in real-time.

We now have the means and the expertise to dynamically align unlimited market segments to a pre-populated platform of resources poised to deploy in real-time across different marketing channels in which content, media selection, and timing are all determined by if/then algorithms triggered by the individual prospect.

That's a mouthful. What are the implications here?

What this means is that we can automatically create ultra-high relevancy, not simply for one group, but for multiple segments, and on an individual, one to one basis without disrupting the core brand positioning.

As we unfold this book, readers will discover what was deemed impossibly inefficient in the area of expense and time to market, relative to increasing new revenue streams from new marketing channels, is now possible, productive, and powerful when we approach the challenge by marshalling the convergence of new technology, which leads to entirely new methodology, yielding entirely new creative and strategic possibilities.

Some at the forefront of the marketing industry have the methodology—not just technology, but also the strategy, the people—to affordably and effectively create the content and deliver the right segmented message to the right person at the right time in the right media channel. That's the power of Neuromarketology™. Read on to understand how it can revolutionize your company's growth.

CHAPTER 1—TAKE AWAYS

- Don't be confounded by the fast moving marketing environment. Instead look closely at the incremental and monumental changes to see which marketing doors open as others close.

CHAPTER 2

Ending the Sacrifice of the Many For the One

Paradigm time!

We've all been at the table for those endless branding and positioning meetings, the ones that seem to lead everywhere and nowhere simultaneously. You know how they play out. Everyone has a different take on what the brand/product offers and to whom. The marketing director sees it one way and the vice president of sales sees it another. The boss has his own perspective and pretty soon, even Legal and your CFO have an opinion, which is always challenging when it comes to marketing.

Then, to resolve the impasse, the whiteboards are rolled out, the colored pens get passed around, the consultant-facilitated exercises kick in, and the buzzwords start to fly. Anything you can think of, in an attempt to bring about consensus and reasonable resolution, is tried. Countless skewed opinions are compiled into neatly disguised research, departmental reports, customer and demographic metrics, as well as the notorious stakeholder anecdotes, and let's not forget those glorious, ever-present "focus groups of one." And what's the worst part of this whole process, especially if it's your job to lead it? Just about everyone is usually right! At least to a degree.

The Diamond on Display

Almost any brand or product/service naturally offers a range of benefits to a variety of prospects and customers. Depending on who they are, and what they're looking for, consumers can be matched to a different brand attribute or feature of a brand/product/service.

A brand is like a diamond. Picture your brand as a diamond whose many facets represent the different points of connection to the potential universe of consumers. You can clearly see how the connection points to the brand or product/service, and to each consumer, are different. Just as

A Brand is Like a Diamond

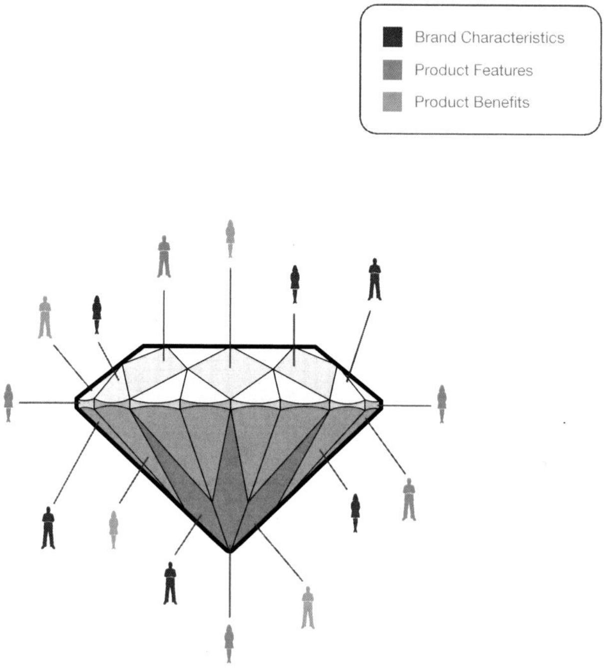

the facets of a diamond refract light differently, the naturally occurring brand attributes or product features reflect differently to different audiences. Within this book, we will discuss how these facets or points of connection can be mapped directly to each potential prospect or customer based on the customer's individual perspectives, desires, and behaviors, collected directly from the customer.

So how do we, as marketers, leverage the varied potential market appeal and associated brand messaging of our brand's *total* possible audience reach without diluting our primary market messaging, strategy, and budgets?

How do we create and deploy marketing that nurtures the comprehensive growth of a brand without delineating one clear message for one definitive audience that concentrates our communications enough to reach the awareness tipping point and prompt action?

After all, conventional wisdom says utilize a single core message strategy that determines the single best claim and promise you can fulfill as an organization, then match it to a core target audience that can be reached efficiently and has the size to sustain the sales growth and goals of the company.

This same strategy, by its very success, also simultaneously casts the brand as a misfit for the plethora of other market share slices to which the brand *could* also appeal.

That old, conventional thinking has been called our best practice marketing strategy for the last fifty years. It has been our dominant marketing theory, our sacred creed. Thou shalt consciously and wholeheartedly eliminate the brand attributes from the messaging and brand essence that naturally exist and that many internal stakeholders know exist and the reports and metrics show exist. Thou shalt instead appeal to "one primary target audience" (and maybe a couple of secondary influencers) that has been ordained as *the one* upon which you shall build your marketing reach.

The obvious and inherent inefficiency of our long-established best practice thinking is that the true *potential* market will never be discovered by the brand if this traditional strategy is deployed.

So how do we, as marketing leaders, bring it all together? How do we turn on or maximize the reach to our primary target audience without turning off the various niche audiences that could also purchase our product at significant levels?

Brand as Beauty Pageant

Traditionally, the answer has been: we can't. So, we don't. Instead, we go through this intensive analytic process of examining the features, benefits, attributes, and our potential marketing claims one by one. We identify them and then we quantify them. We categorize them and then qualify them. We line them up and run them through our branding best practices filter, and then—are you ready?

We start dismissing them. We dismiss one unquestionably accurate, intrinsic, and powerful brand quality after another. Not because they are not valid or the vice president of sales does not understand the finer points of marketing, but because under conventional wisdom, and based on legacy-level technology platforms, only one claim, only one essential message (with maybe a key sub-message or two squeezed in along with it) can be the winner. It's like a beauty pageant where the highly attractive attributes get sent off stage one by one until a single message emerges that stands out above all the rest—"Here she comes, Miss America!"—the key brand message, with its unique selling point and singular brand attribute, that will hit the single biggest market slice you have identified that your brand has the qualities to support.

Getting back to the often endless internal branding debate, it's not that the operations guy was wrong or the vice president of customer relations or the CEO or even Legal. The brand *does* naturally speak uniquely to different people, and those differences are accelerated based on the individuals' environmental conditions or progression in the buying cycle.

What's at Play Here is the Sacrifice of the Many for the One

This sacred dance of positioning has been the essence and common denominator of all great marketing for the last four decades. In their seminal work, *Positioning: The Battle for Your Mind*, Trout and Ries changed marketing forever by declaring that you can't just tell people to buy; you have to show them that the product is right for them. By establishing this affinity, you can influence people to desire your product and then you realize your highest return on your marketing investments.

Ever since then, the great minds of marketing have turned themselves to the task of discovering and developing that singular relevancy in messaging that will make any given product feel perfectly right *to the largest number of people*.

Find the *one*, and winnow out everything else. Zero in on the *single* message that best conveys your brand to the exclusion of all others. And then you've got the keys to the kingdom—you've got the magic element that will propel your brand to its peak of popularity and profitability. It has been a high art and a deep science, a combination of exceptionally thoughtful strategy and the bold, brash roll of the dice based on others' experiences.

And what does the traditional sacrifice of the many for the one get you? The hope of a 2 percent return (if you're lucky), assuming the strategy is on the mark and the execution is professional. Two percent. That's what all the blood, sweat, and bruising debate is all about. All the discussion and analysis of *what we offer* and *who we offer it to.* All the positioning and repositioning and post-positioning. All the getting it right and getting it wrong and doing it anyway. It comes down to chasing a fleeting 2 percent return on your marketing investment.

The following illustration makes it graphically clear that when we focus on the one, we miss 98 percent of potential prospects.

The Sacrifice of the Many for the One

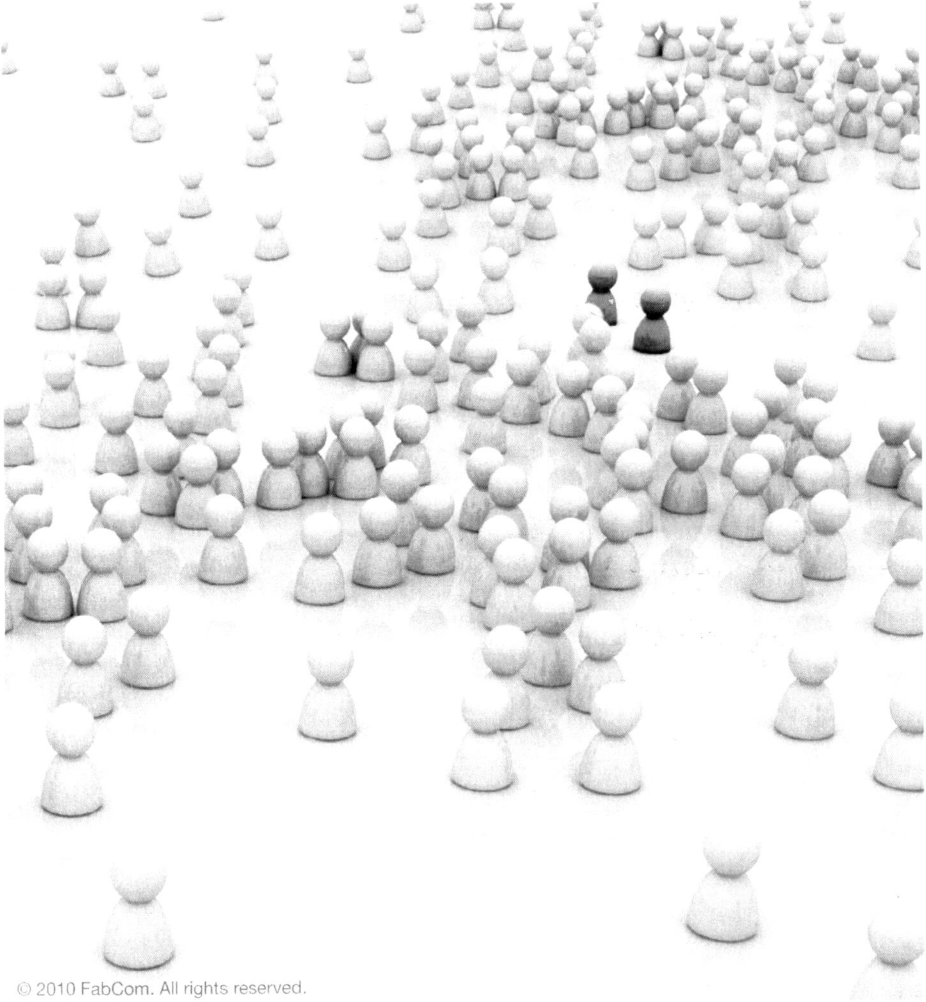

Marketers intentionally pass up the 98 percent in order to make solid contact with the 2 percent we determine are the most likely to convert into customers.

The Ignored Majority

All this begs the question: what happened to the remaining 98 percent, who offered no response whatsoever? The ignored majority. As we all know, if we follow the conventional wisdom of homing in on your one core audience and the singularity of brand attributes they are most likely to respond to at the expense of all others, we intentionally pass up the 98 percent. Traditional marketing strategy has dictated: In order to make solid contact with the 2 percent or less that we as marketers have determined are most likely to convert into customers, we must turn a blind eye to other perfectly good customers. We sacrificed the natural and inarguable relevancies to the various groups making up that 98 percent in order to hit our target audience straight and hard, in order to arrive at that single positioning most likely to succeed with the single group most likely to be receptive. Conventional wisdom demands we concentrate our media, sales efforts, and organizational resources at the minority that are most likely to respond.

"The One to One Future" is Now

In their groundbreaking 1993 book, *The One to One Future*, Don Peppers and Martha Rogers were the first marketing theorists to stress the importance of extreme segmentation and personalization in successful marketing—essentially making a unique offering of a product or service to each prospect and customer. They stressed that marketers had to understand the customer's point of view, behaviors, and perceptions and use that knowledge as the foundation for marketing communication.

But that was nearly twenty years ago—before we had unified email, Google, Wi-Fi or broadband Internet, social media, dynamically accessible databases, or an entire economy revolving around 24/7, perpetually connected two-way communication devices. While it was a revolutionary concept that has proven to be a very valuable insight, it was economically impossible to fully implement the concept except for those with public company timelines and budgets, until very recently.

Today, this is no longer merely a theoretical insight. Nor is it a best practice that only the biggest can afford. Now it is possible to fully realize the potential of one to one marketing because newly available technology allows you to develop the same knowledge about each of your customers and/or prospects—whether hundreds or millions of them. This new capability that allows dynamically generated *dialogue* within your marketing provides the platform for a mutual and real-time marketing relationship upon which you can build brand success and sales.

In a very real sense, you can now have the same sort of relevant, interactive relationship with huge numbers of customers with the kind of relevance and timing that only mom and pop stores or the best corporate salespeople could develop through face-to-face contact. That means dynamically segmenting audiences, communicating individually and personally resonating with each member—all automatically and instantaneously. In the next chapter, we'll discuss this in greater detail and show how a whole new generation of segmentation strategy is now not only a possibility, but a necessity.

CHAPTER 2—TAKE AWAYS

- Like the many facets of a diamond, your brand has multiple points of connection/attributes that *can* be mapped and connected to all your targets individually.
- As opposed to conventional wisdom, the brand does naturally speak uniquely to different people, and those differences are accelerated based on individuals' environmental conditions or progression in the buying cycle. Now that we embrace this concept, consider how it changes your messaging.
- Do not accept a 98 percent failure rate. Ask why your marketing campaign failed to reach and spur reaction to 98 percent of the people you targeted. Seek a better return using a neuromarketing strategy and one to one dynamic marketing.

CHAPTER 3

Not Your Daddy's Segmentation

The dynamic segmentation edge

"Yes, we understand market segmentation. We do segmentation. We buy our media and sort our lists and place our ads and/or assign sales and support teams according to our target audiences. We would love to create another marketing division or product extension as a sure-fire way to more sales, but we can't afford that on our budget."

Or:

"It takes years, as well as public-money kind of budgets, and patience to develop those additional channels (conventional wisdom based on conventional marketing process and methodology). *I don't have years to develop an approach and marketing support for new market channels. I need new sales from what I have or can afford now."*

As the CEO of a mid-sized, full-service, integrated marketing agency, serving clients large and small nationwide for two decades, I hear a version of these two statements most often when first meeting a client and introducing our alternative thinking.

But what if the sacrifice of the possibility of the many for the probability of the few was not a hard and fast law? What if you could fish in multiple ponds at one time instead of just the one? What if you could present your product as a great choice for *this* audience, and separately, as a great choice for *that* audience? This would mean you could increase your relevance for each group and reasonably expect a fair return from each and every pool of sequentially targeted prospects, rather than having to write those market segments off from the get-go.

Great idea, but not a new one, right? It's called segmentation and it's been around for quite a while. If you could attain relevance in *all* of your potential market segments, you know you could conservatively double your business. All well and good as a concept, but as seasoned marketers know, the human resources required to develop that many approaches, and the technological capability to parse the messaging, represent daunting challenges. Bottom line: the idea is good, but in practice, if configured from the existing legacy technology platforms and conventional methodology, your costs would go through the roof. Common sense says this type of an approach can only provide the needed return on investment for those with the deepest pockets.

The problem with conventional segmentation is that it's expensive enough to develop and deploy *one* great campaign, which is what it takes to move the needle these days, much less to attempt marketing effectiveness across multiple segments, including the one to one dynamic messaging needed to create multiple comprehensive campaign experiences per prospect group. As high as the costs to develop and build multiple effective campaigns can be, they are only one element of the segmentation spending equation. The other is media. Purchasing the media in which to deploy the multiple campaigns and varied flightings required to reach different target markets has traditionally come with too steep a price tag for any but the biggest brands to pay.

Using traditional process and thinking, there is a perception challenge when considering capacity. Most marketers are challenged to get their monthly campaigns out to a single segment, much less to many. This is because most are utilizing virtually the same production methodology they've used since the dawn of desktop publishing decades ago.

The Segmentation Pay-off

Those who *can* afford developing multiple market segments achieve phenomenal results. The segmentation strategy has proven itself as a bellweather for more than a century and is deployed by larger brands almost universally. This kind of marketing can cost an additional 50 percent over the cost of developing a single segment of customers, but has been proven to consistently deliver 200 percent-plus in ongoing returns by channeling multiple new revenue streams into those companies.

Microsoft, a company that knows something about market share, targets business users, home users, and IT professionals, segmenting each of these areas by type. They further segment their business user audience by scale, from small and mid-size companies to enterprise organizations. Microsoft also segments by industry, including education, financial services, government, retail, and eight other industry focuses. Several of these are sub-segmented as well, such as education, which addresses K-12 audiences and higher education audiences separately.

Where would Microsoft be if they only focused on one of these many audiences? If they had settled on that one message that resonated the most to that one group? Obviously, just a fraction of the company they are today. Now, imagine the branding process they would have to go through to arrive at that one. It would be insanity up in Redmond, WA, a corporate bloodbath in which the best and the brightest tear each other to pieces. Fortunately, they can afford not to sacrifice the many for the one.

Another example is MetLife, you know, the "Snoopy" insurance company. Snoopy sells to individuals, businesses, brokers, and consultants. Individuals are segmented by age, income, and lifestyle. And on and on. Again, where would Snoopy be if he marketed to retirement-minded heads of families at the expense of business group benefits and all the company's other revenue streams? Hard to say for sure, but it is clear that he wouldn't be the big dog that he is—one of America's largest insurers.

Let's Get Real

Comparing traditional segmentation to dynamic segmentation is like comparing arithmetic to differential equations.

What about those who think they can't afford the luxury of true segmentation and the proven return it provides? When we consider that segmentation is akin to mathematics as a subject, we can start to see some of the hidden potential. Segmentation, as a strategy, has many nuances in its creation and implementation. Its true power belongs to those who have invested a lifetime in studying the applications and can apply the deeper and more granular nuances to solve even the most daunting of communication challenges.

Most understand the power and variable ability to solve problems of mathematics, depending on which process is used and the experience of practitioners using the process. Think eighth grade mathematics versus nuclear physics. They both use mathematics to solve a problem. They both use multiplication, division, addition, and subtraction at some point in the process.

But it's obvious that solving a multiplication problem is not the same as completing a quadratic equation. When you think about it, those same mathematical intermediate calculations are used and added to other deeper thinking processes only by the most experienced and innovative mathematicians. These math wizards use the commonly known math, *plus* defined complicated formulas to solve problems in ways most of us who do not understand complex mathematics could not imagine.

It is simple to see a physics equation for the first time and say, "I can do that" because it starts with known processes. Similarly, it is simple to say, when introduced to *dynamic* marketing and the resulting new methodology of hyper-relevant messaging, "We're already doing that." "We divide by our target audiences, we multiply our chances by running targeted media, we subtract the competitors' offers to ensure our offer outperforms, and we add in a little online marketing. We can do, and are doing, dynamic personalized and cross-channel marketing."

As we continue to unfold the individual pieces that, when added together, become a sum exponentially more than the total of their parts, please keep your mind open to the analogy above and the difference between simple math and the use of simple math in more dynamic equations. This accurately describes the relationship between dynamic segmentation and conventional segmentation as we know it.

We commonly find that certain personalities with less experience in an emerging area will use whatever means possible to protect their position and deny the need for any outside insight or updating of practices. When confronted with new concepts beyond their comfort zone, they tend to fake it, they ignore it, or they dismiss it based on some perceived unique characteristic of their company or situation.

Segmentation strategy is the foundation for most sophisticated marketers. Simply attracting more customers that introduce greater diversity into the sales funnel creates more revenue and more stability. The only question in the past for smart marketers when considering deploying segmentation as a marketing strategy was: "Can my company afford the time and money that it typically and historically has taken with conventional processes to open up and project my brand messaging to multiple market segments simultaneously?"

We will share with you a way to accomplish the reach and relevancy of dynamic segmentation with completely new methodology that uses completely different and compounded thinking compared to conventional and entrenched marketing processes. We will demonstrate in this book the "how" and "what" that make up the differences between the way we have, as an industry, deployed segmentation in the past and what is available to you now. Our objective is to help the small to mid-size marketer deploy dynamic cross-media, cross-channel, personalized marketing *automatically* across all potential targets and help lead the large companies to a more efficient process that will raise existing efforts to new heights of success, reach, and return on investment.

Just as importantly, in matters of change, we will outline the restraining forces both from a technology and human resource perspective. As marketing leaders, we know that reactions of the personnel involved can make or break an initiative, especially if they do not know how, or feel they do not have the resources, to deploy what is the best practices solution.

Introducing the new methodology of dynamic marketing and Neuromarketology™ feels to me like déjà vu from the early days when we were introducing the Internet to our customers as a marketing engine. We would discuss with clients creating a web presence and the resulting enormous opportunity. Frequently back then, we would hear, "we are already getting online" or "we are doing that in-house" or "we have an initiative for that going now."

Creating a web presence based on our early lead in the industry meant, to us, securing their brands' and sub-brands' URLs. The thinking was totally different from thinking used when naming a catalog or product. We understood through years of early deployment that creating searchable organic content would allow them, as early adopters, to be found through search engines before their competitors were found by the millions of new potential customers logging online every day. We were recommending getting their storefronts up, getting their click-and-order processes online, as well as their customer service functions. We knew we needed to build different content, different calls to action, and different production processes. As early adopters and leaders, we had already invested two years learning the entire methodology of creation, and implementation had to be different from traditional campaign or direct mail development.

Inevitably, when we peeled away the onion and discussed exactly what clients were implementing, this is how it often played out:

Many companies did have an initiative to get online. They would put up a static web page. It was, well, simply static. It had no functionality. It did not lower their operational costs. It did not emotionally appeal to their target audience and sell more of their products or services. They had basically created and were satisfied for the first couple of years with a placebo online presence that squandered the company's future potential.

This sort of implementation, or what we call in the advertising business "kung fu implementation," is much more devastating to a company than just a stakeholder defending their efforts or buying time to figure it out on their own. This behavior has a long-term debilitating effect on the executives' abilities to see the early returns from a new or emerging channel and adjust corporate strategy to provide more resources. Early foresight and transparency are critical to companies. They allow leaders to direct the company to enjoy more easily attained gains before their competitors do. The laws of adoption, as well as the laws of supply and demand, will always conspire against the slow to react, driving the cost for late adopters to levels that make market entry painful and resource-depleting.

This seemingly innocuous internal protectionism manifests itself commonly in stakeholders who easily dismiss the difference of what *could* be accomplished by a new capability and instead focus on what *they are* accomplishing. It is the simple difference of thinking about what can *actually* be accomplished versus what some *perceive* can be accomplished. The associated long-term side effect from this type of behavior retarded many companies' ability from the get-go in the new Internet economy.

The self-piloted, "let's give it a try with what we know and what we have" approach rarely led to success. It did not provide an additional portal to outflank competitors and connect to a larger share of the market. This behavior, by default, buys time to go through the budget cycles and years of appeasement for top management before the existing team members can acquire the knowledge and the resources to implement properly. This is usually brought to a head after news reports and studies are widely available to create the pressure to adopt. When those data points are combined with the lessening effectiveness of old models, majority adoption kicks in.

The result for many organizations that waited for proof of majority adoption to be served up by the mainstream? Months and years passed before they started capturing the gains of the new Internet economy. If they had just opened their minds to what could be different about an area like marketing that they knew so well, they *could* have led their company to great gains based on their existing budgets and position. They *could* have acquired new markets utilizing the resources and knowledge of the market leaders at the time. The low hanging fruit went to those who adopted the new methodology. The organizations that adopted early and thoughtfully ran away with the ring in the '90s and the first ten years of this century. Our message to marketers large and small: if you wait for this new methodology to become mainstream or wait to assimilate the resources and expertise, then you will miss the boat. (This same phenomenon happened when we introduced desktop publishing and the first Macintosh in the Southwest—but that story is told later in the book.)

The bottom line: don't let your company go through this very expensive cycle. I'm writing this book because those of us ages 40 to 55 have had three of these game-changing revolutions during our careers. We should be getting good at it by now. The first was desktop publishing; the second was the advent of the Internet; and now, dynamic segmentation and the resulting new methodology. We have an opportunity, as marketing leaders, to absorb the early and late adoption principles and lead our companies to extraordinary gains. To do this, we must harness the power of the breakthroughs in dynamic one to one marketing before our competitors figure it out and drive up the cost of entry by scraping away the low hanging fruit.

The good news: most of us have already started down the path of assembling the *basic* elements of dynamic workflows that pave the way for greater marketing gains in the new consumer-centric economy.

The Framework

The overall concept of digital workflow efficiency and capability is not foreign. By now, most marketers understand how the connectivity of digital files can offer efficiency to their marketing efforts. An example, we all know, is digital repurposing.

We define the one image you know everyone in your various audiences will respond to—let's say it's a picture of a puppy and a little girl. Who could resist that?

To build out the campaign and control your costs, you use it across all media. Your puppy/little girl image appears in the online ad, the TV commercial, the HTML newsletter, and in your print campaign.

While you don't have to pay for a new image each time, barring usage rights, you do have an expense to bear when it comes to preparing the image for each application. Your e-commerce team wants the file as a JPEG at 72 dpi, and then manipulates it in SQL to be called from a database. Your printer needs to work the file over with InDesign and adjust the resolution to 300 dpi for print. Your website team wants the file in Photoshop and will rework it in their web layout application. And let's not forget the video crew who need to completely rework the image in Avid or a vector application at NTSC specifications.

Shuffling that same image between completely different teams with different skills, working in different software for different applications, costs money. By the time you're done, you've paid five times for different teams of specialists to prepare that central campaign image of the little girl and her puppy for the various applications. That's only one image within your campaign! This goes on and on in publishing. The waste of the conventional marketing processes and workflows is multiplied by each line of copy, each headline, each product line, each supplier, and so on.

Not surprisingly, half-way measures yield half-way results. You can realize significant savings when deploying content aggregation initiatives, as well as the added bonus of content control. However, the real exponential returns come when this basic digital workflow process can be linked to an end-to-end, real-time, dynamic electronic publishing methodology. That's when you bring it all together and can tap into the real production efficiencies of a technologically converged environment.

Don't worry; the purpose of this book is to detail this emerging methodology and the new dynamic workflow so that the buzzwords stop buzzing. The content aggregation initiative implemented by the larger in-house marketing departments and best-of-class agencies years ago is just the tip of the iceberg when linked with the newest breakthroughs in one to one dynamic marketing.

Aggregation Aggravation

Unless you've got deep, deep pockets, the strain on budgets and resources to effectively implement a dynamic marketing and one to one segmentation strategy under conventional circumstances and without the newest methodology will inevitably force you right back into the same old conundrum. Conventional wisdom says you can't afford to hit all the markets, so you've got to prioritize. Where do you get your best ROI? *That's* where you put your money. Whichever segment or segments we choose, inevitably, we know we will consciously disregard large numbers of people who map directly to some of our brand attributes in order to make the proverbial sacrifice of the many for the one. This drives us right back to the 2 percent or less model. It's like a law of nature—we can't seem to get around it. Or can we?

A new methodology is now available, which has been in the works for decades, with leaders in various fields exploring, implementing, improving, testing, and redeploying over time. Enabled fully by new technology, this methodology seamlessly links the sound brand strategy of the past with the collective power of database, dialogue, and personalized variable dynamic marketing within any channel to establish a new paradigm in selling success.

This methodology provides the platform for reaching customers and prospects on a true one to one basis, meaning the right message, at the right moment, to the right audience, delivered in the right media. The result is marketing relevance that is so permeating that it drives total marketing ROI off the charts.

Relevance for All

The ability to deliver hyper-relevance consistently and affordably frees you from the traditional tried and true mass marketing equation. In the simplest terms, instead of needing to send out one hundred identical generic marketing messages to receive the hope of two responses, you can now send just ten to receive one response. Why? Because you're speaking directly to that specific segment's interests on a truly personalized and relevant manner determined by their own preferences and hierarchy of needs.

Now take those other ninety marketing messages/touches or resources you were going to use in the conventional one to many methodology to get your 2 percent response, and deploy them instead within nine more market segments. This methodology enables you to map brand attributes into all your potential segments and markets rather than focusing on just one or a few.

Again, ultra-high emotional relevance is essential. We're not talking about simply using a personalized name or blue for men and pink for women. A successful one to one dynamic marketer must develop and deploy dynamic dialogue mechanisms that include online and offline interactive and engaging "sticky" tools designed to facilitate the collection of detailed information and user priorities, and that are automatically collected in real-time within information groupings relative to the prospect and your brand, product, or service attributes. This dynamically- and user-generated collection of information provides the multiple criteria levels necessary to achieve both hyper-relevance and superb timing with your marketing.

Once this information profile is collected, it can be used to drive numerous contacts within that prospective grouping. This same messaging can be shared with the prospect or customer in real-time across all communication platforms and all interaction points with your brand.

Advanced if/then strategic thinking and then tactical programming determines which image is used, which copy, which call to action, and how and when the messaging is presented.

As a result of this new hyper-relevance, it can take only ten outbound marketing messages to gain your one respondent. Now repeat this process in each of ten segments for an ROI of ten total responses versus the conventional outcome of two responses from the original group of one hundred exposed to one to many messaging.

Here's an illustration of the results that can be achieved when we deploy this methodology:

One to Many vs. One to One Targeted Methodology

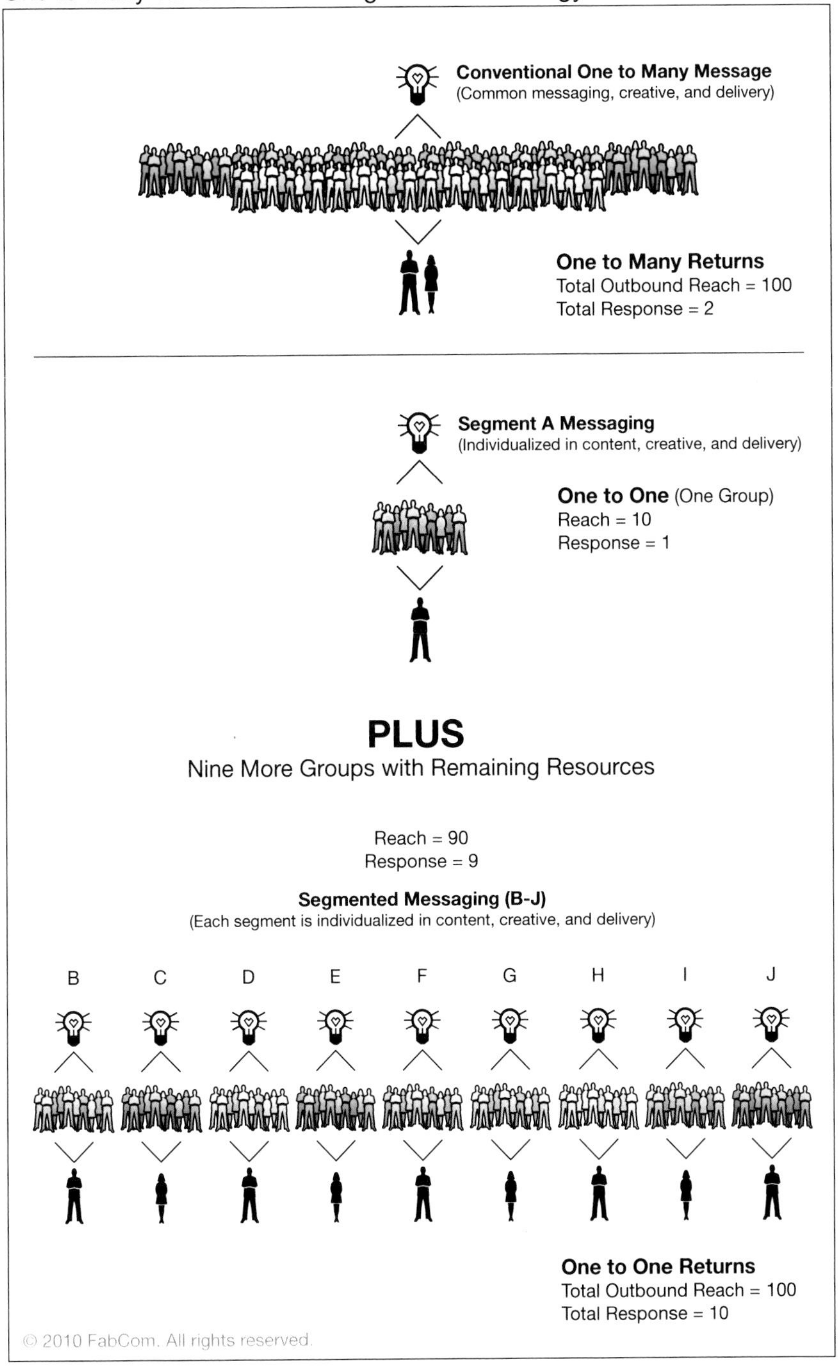
Conventional One to Many Message
(Common messaging, creative, and delivery)
One to Many Returns
Total Outbound Reach = 100
Total Response = 2
Segment A Messaging
(Individualized in content, creative, and delivery)
One to One (One Group)
Reach = 10
Response = 1
PLUS
Nine More Groups with Remaining Resources
Reach = 90
Response = 9
Segmented Messaging (B-J)
(Each segment is individualized in content, creative, and delivery)
B C D E F G H I J
One to One Returns
Total Outbound Reach = 100
Total Response = 10
© 2010 FabCom. All rights reserved.

Welcome to Neuromarketology™

So, where does this leave us? Suddenly you've been catapulted from that 2 percent response to a 10 percent response. You are a genius, you are a hero, and you are a practitioner of neuromarketing.

Neuromarketology™ is the study of reactions driven from the core brain based on the exposure to specific marketing messages, imagery, and timing. It's the science of knowing each of your target audience's emotional connection points and methodology of configuring your marketing messages to connect your brand attributes with each stakeholder in the most relevant manner for that specific target.

When deploying this new methodology, we are no longer sacrificing the many for the few. Rather, we are pinpointing those brand attributes that viscerally move the mind of your consumers across a range of segments, on a legitimate, authentic one to one basis. Once you make this paradigm shift, the methodology that cascades from Neuromarketology™ enables ongoing communication through a dynamic one to one dialogue with your customers in the place and manner of their choosing.

Whether it's a print piece for a senior at home, a text message to a teenager, or a robust online offer for a Baby Boomer, the point is, *they* pick the brand attributes, time, and channel through which *they* most want to interact.

Now, integrate the multiple marketing channels available today from TV's new interactive capability, social networking, interactive online portals, the proliferation of interactive real-time connected personal communication devices, and beyond. These are amazing two-way dialogue platforms through which your brand can interact with consumers. You can leverage all these media including Facebook, blogs, offline event communities, and whatever media channel is coming next, to carry your dynamic, database-driven communications directly to each recipient in your segmented audiences the way they want to receive them.

The illustration on the next page shows how each of the many facets of a brand can be tied to individual prospects and customers who have a particular affinity for specific brand elements.

Conventional Marketing Wisdom
One to Many Methodology

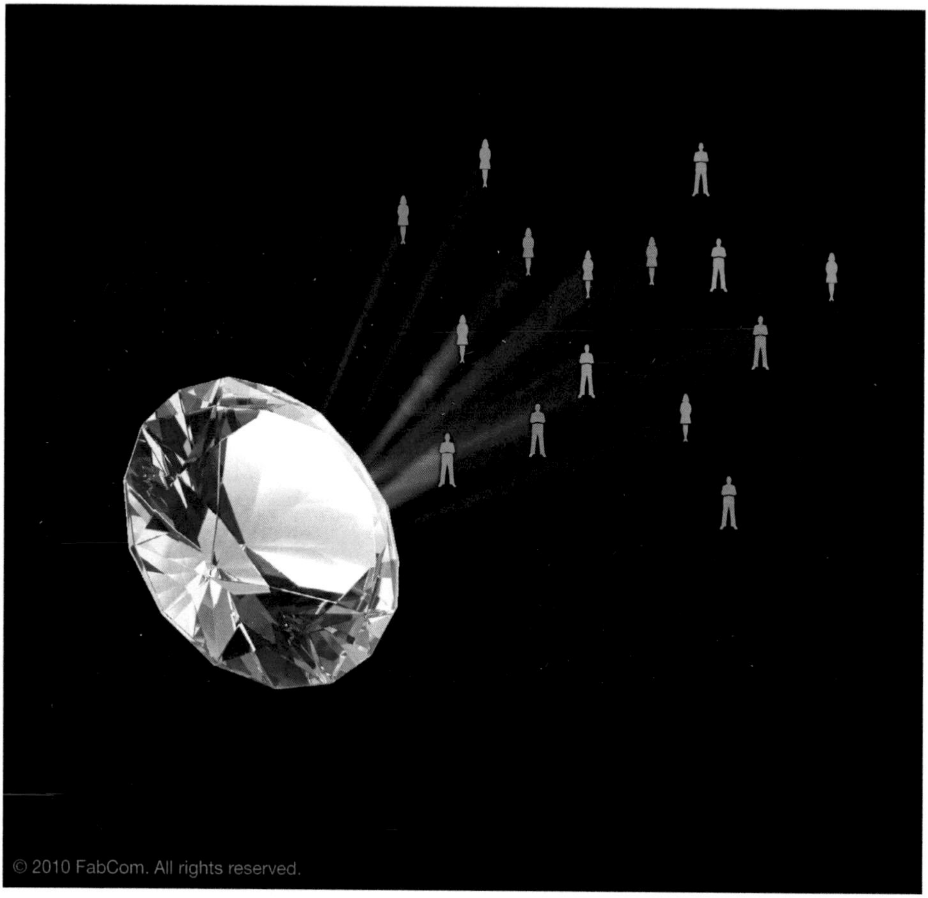
© 2010 FabCom. All rights reserved.

By ignoring the brand's many facets, by following a single messaging and consolidated targeting strategy, we intentionally pass on marketing the many connection points of the brand that can authentically attract a wide variety of consumers.

Neuromarketology™ Mapping

Dynamic One to One Segmentation Methodology

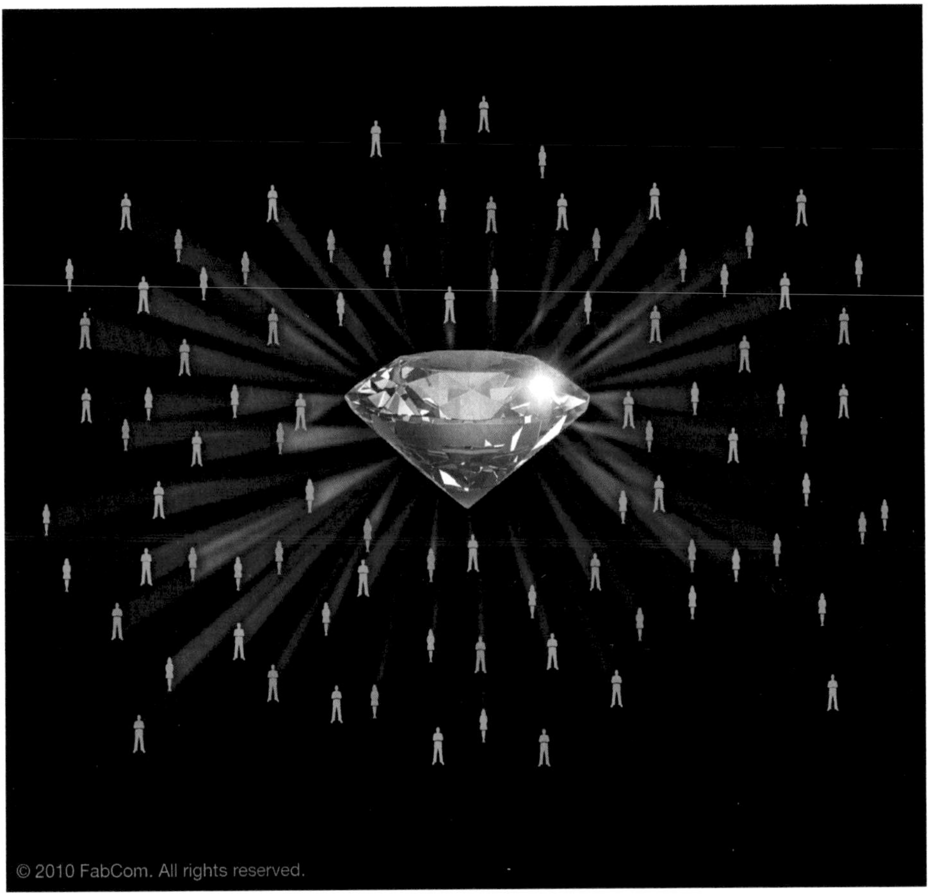
© 2010 FabCom. All rights reserved.

The results of deploying neuromarketing and mapping your brand attributes directly to individual prospects dynamically and creating a natural alignment between your customers needs and the facets of your brand.

But, beware of brand dilution! Many organizations are not taking the new and emerging communication channels seriously enough. They are handing off the responsibility for communicating through these channels to their IT and other support staff. Many have limited understanding of what the company positioning is and how to map the brand attributes honestly and accurately into the new channels utilizing the demographics, psychographics, and behavioral attributes of your targets.

In other words, we are seeing many examples of project teams driving their brands off a cliff. In an attempt to drive messaging with content management systems—the forefather of this methodology—many are turning their brands into vanilla. They are dispersing content and imagery that is slowly but surely transforming their brands into commodities, deteriorating conversion rates, and taxing their lead generation budgets. Many implementations of content management systems, in an attempt to manage the messaging are, in actuality, watering down the messaging.

They are utilizing templates with diluted, unconnected messaging that happen to be the same templates (look, feel, and interaction) their competitors deploy. The attempt to manage the content can become the great neutralizer to all brand, advertising, and sales development efforts.

Here is a quick summary of a classic situation:

A company is driving leads with marketing that emotionally involves the prospects enough to respond, but then they fail to convert the leads into relationships with the sales team, at the call centers, or at online sales portals. When we take a deeper look and diagnose the fall off in conversions, the majority of the time we find that the differentiating and clear messaging designed to progress the sale stops at the most important and expensive point in the process. We find the online portals, forms, call centers, and sales interactions that cause conversion are sterilized of the emotional fiber and differentiating characteristics that drove leads to respond in the first place. As marketers, we must constantly be vigilant stewards of what exactly holds together the decision to purchase or invest and of exactly what the customer needs to progress through the buying cycle.

Just because the methodology has evolved, this doesn't mean we can afford to ignore the brand positioning dictums of Trout and Ries. The fundamentals of branding according to Trout and Ries still hold true. In fact, in this incredibly cluttered and diversified communications marketplace, your brand integrity is more critical than ever.

You still must tell people why you are the best choice for them and distinguish your brand from others. The difference is that now, within this new methodology, we can strategically map *all* relevant and powerful brand attributes to multiple market segments simultaneously at all levels of customer interaction, no matter how divergent, based on if/then programming.

Is this a challenge in terms of time and resources? Absolutely, but once you've laid the groundwork, you've done it. Your end-to-end marketing system is configured and ready to execute at extremely high performance levels. After that, it's just a matter of measuring, tracking, and refining. Ask yourself this question before you read on: which approach (the traditional or the new) promises a greater return on my investment?

CHAPTER 3—TAKE AWAYS

- Segmentation is a time-tested marketing strategy. Keep in mind, conventional approaches relinquish the ability to implement successful segmentation strategies to the largest of budgets. By utilizing a dynamic, one to one marketing methodology, you can create at least a fivefold monthly return on invested marketing dollars. Use technology, innovation, and creativity to develop multiple channels of revenues simultaneously into your organization.

- Use the concepts presented in *Neuromarketology* to map your true and complete brand attributes directly to each and every unique customer desire and strive to increase your market reach by a number of at least ten.

- Be on the lookout for brand dilution. These kinds of evolutionary changes lead most to believe they can piecemeal implementation, but if this approach is allowed to infiltrate your initiative, then the messaging will not be dynamically connected to achieve the hyper relevance that creates the significant difference in returns.

CHAPTER 4

A Holistic Strategy for a Whole Food

Neuromarketology™ in action

We recently worked with a nutritional supplement product derived from freshwater single-celled green algae. This green algae is organically loaded with naturally-occurring vitamins and antioxidants including: vitamin C, pro-vitamin A (beta-carotene), chlorophyll, lutein, thiamine (B1), riboflavin (B2), pyridoxine (B6), niacin, and several more.

When the client came to us, they were limiting their marketing reach to seniors aged seventy-plus. Seniors made up the segment where they had the most success. But a product with this many powerful ingredients had to offer a wide range of benefits that could be relevant to many segments. Before we started a single creative initiative, we conducted secondary research through the FDA to find out what claims we could legally make for the product based on its amazing overall nutritional value. Not surprisingly, we were able to identify an extensive list of categories for which the supplement company could legitimately claim benefits according to the FDA, based on its documented nutritional values, including:

- Anti-Aging
- Weight Loss
- Energy & Fitness
- Wellness
- Heart Health
- Brain Health
- Digestion Health
- Eye Health
- Stress and Mood
- Detoxification
- Joint Health
- Sexual Health

The traditional marketing methodology required the client to forgo most of these attributes and the sub-audiences they could serve in order to reach the group most likely to purchase the highest volume. Many times they also fell into the common trap of trying to communicate all of these attributes on each and every message. Instead of staying with this traditional approach, we developed a strategy that mapped all of these various benefit areas to the audiences for which they were most relevant. For instance, Heart Health for seniors, Anti-Aging for Baby Boomers, and Energy and Fitness for twenty- and thirty-somethings.

We then developed a network of microsites, each one designed to promote a particular set of benefits to one audience segment, as illustrated on pages 48-49.

These microsites/entry portals provided conditional and age group relevance to engage each segment further. Rather than sending prospects to the one primary website that sacrificed the many brand attributes, and thus wider target audiences for the few messages believed supportable for the single target audience as an alternative, we first directed prospective consumers to microsites designed to achieve ultra-high relevance per condition within demographic and behavioral groupings. This strategy assured a positive response to the prospective customer's magic question and a solution to the online shopper's three-second rule: "Is this right for me? Is this what I want, need, or have been looking for?" Target and keyword-rich site names were developed, such as 65plus<heartcondition>.com for seniors, or superfood<dietcondition>.com for younger adults, were selected for their relevance.

For our dynamic marketing strategy, we needed to know our prospects on a one to one basis. To achieve this, we had to create interactivity that would stimulate the consumer dialogue with the brand. We developed and equipped each site and advertising initiative with "sticky tools" that were engaging and customer-centric. The sticky tools were customer-interactive experiences laced within all the communication channels that traded information that the consumer was motivated to provide based on what they received in exchange—a nutritional recipe, a pH test kit, finding a naturopathic doctor in their area, etc. We developed fifteen in all to reach each of the segments we'd identified. (Remember, previously this client was primarily engaging with *one* segment. The strategy broadened their reach to effectively contact consumers in fourteen additional market segments.)

The sticky mechanisms enabled us to gather in-depth information from prospective consumers, far beyond simply capturing their contact information. For example, we developed a "Nutritional Configurator," which provided users with a snapshot of their unique nutritional requirements and personal recommendations for nutritional supplements as needed. To use it, participants needed to input information about themselves such as their age, gender, level of nutritional supplementation, dietary information, and health concerns. All together, this provided us with an extensive personalized profile for that prospective consumer. This information grouping, input by

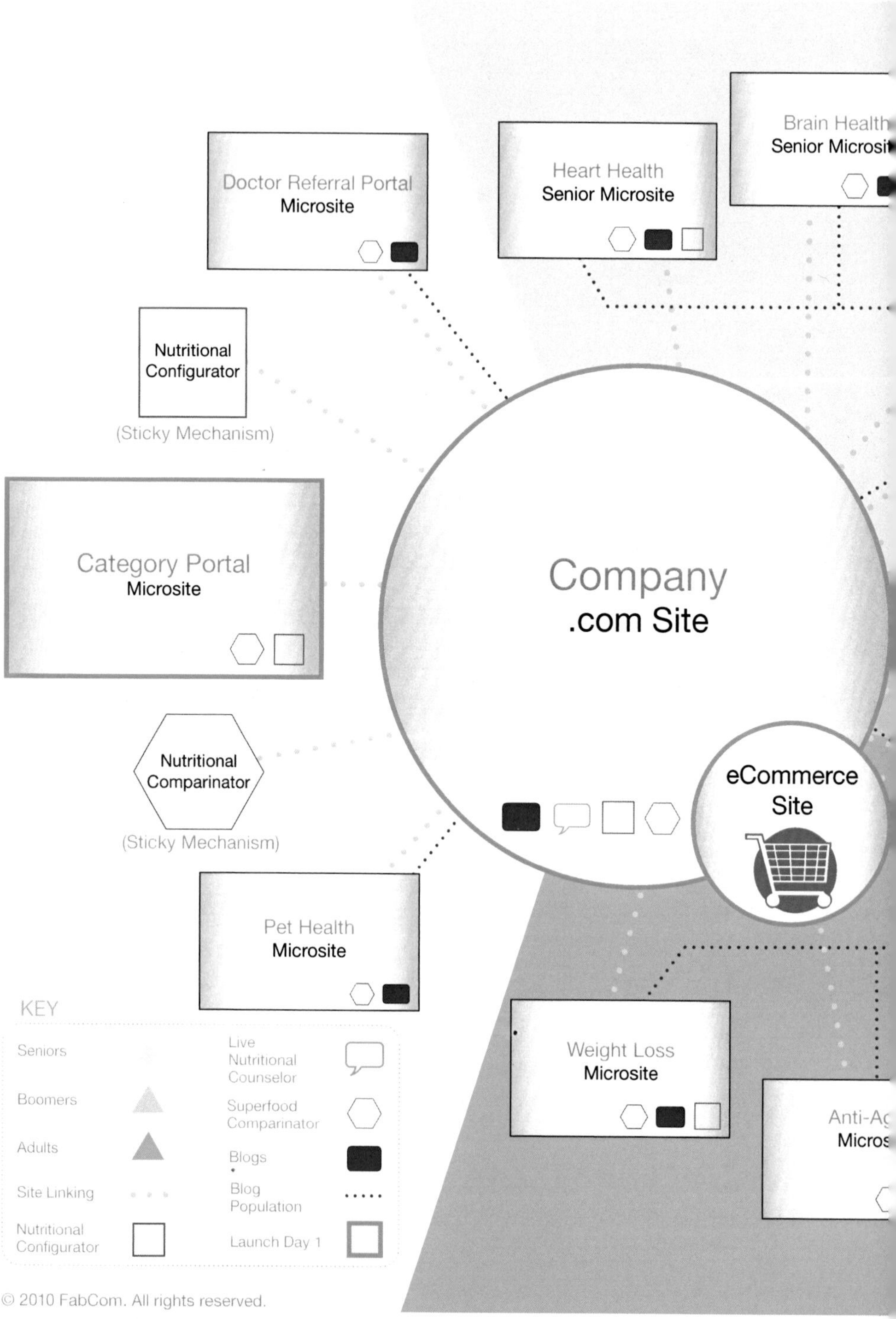

Doctor Referral Portal
Microsite
Heart Health
Senior Microsite
Brain Health
Senior Microsit
Nutritional
Configurator
(Sticky Mechanism)
Category Portal
Microsite
Company
.com Site
Nutritional
Comparinator
(Sticky Mechanism)
eCommerce
Site
Pet Health
Microsite
Weight Loss
Microsite
Anti-Ag
Micros
KEY
Seniors
Boomers
Adults
Site Linking
Nutritional
Configurator
Live
Nutritional
Counselor
Superfood
Comparinator
Blogs
Blog
Population
Launch Day 1

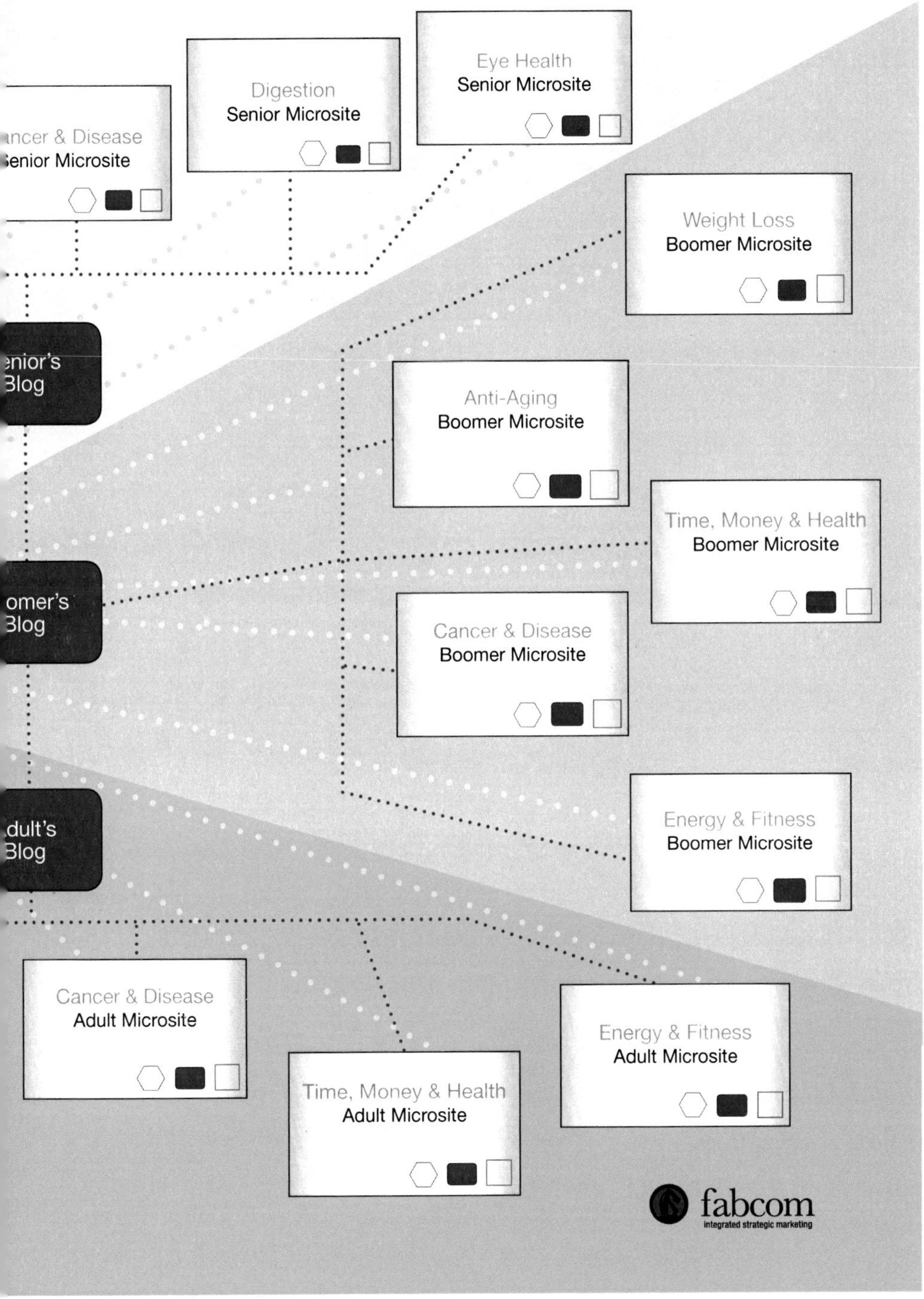
Eye Health
Senior Microsite
Digestion
Senior Microsite
ancer & Disease
Senior Microsite
Weight Loss
Boomer Microsite
enior's
Blog
Anti-Aging
Boomer Microsite
Time, Money & Health
Boomer Microsite
omer's
Blog
Cancer & Disease
Boomer Microsite
Energy & Fitness
Boomer Microsite
dult's
Blog
Cancer & Disease
Adult Microsite
Energy & Fitness
Adult Microsite
Time, Money & Health
Adult Microsite
fabcom
integrated strategic marketing

the prospects themselves, became the foundation for on-going dialogue marketing, both online and offline.

In addition, this entire targeting and retention strategy was integrated offline through a newly developed "Nutritional Coach" program rolled out with the contact center. Here's where the if/then programming kicks in. *If* you're a fifty-something male whose major concern is digestion and your level of supplementation is moderate and you eat one-to-two servings of fiber daily and you exercise three times a week, *then* you, the prospect, will receive messaging, imagery, and calls to actions that speak directly to your needs and personal perspective. Now, that's high relevance.

The marketing tactics, including unique copy, imagery, offer, and other variables, were automatically assembled from a pre-populated resource pool to map dynamically to product attributes and the consumer's specific health concerns. All secondary funnels from the marketing campaign routed a customer to a PURL (personalized URL) that was anchored by the previously mentioned microsites that were mapped directly to the facet of the product that matched that consumer's reason to purchase.

If we have a senior who is concerned about eye health and heart disease, *then* we send them a piece of direct mail at home that guides them to a dynamically-populated microsite that offers them the perfect solution with images of seniors and content about the combination of heart and eye health concerns.

Conversely, *if* another female senior was sent direct mail at home that spoke to her specific concerns of brain health and energy, *then* she would be directed to a site featuring feminine imagery and the appropriate messaging that relates to her concerns and the product-specific ability to meet those specific concerns.

If we had Baby Boomers with digestion, energy, and fitness concerns, *then* we sent them an HTML and PURL link to a site automatically populated with content that was specific and visceral to these topics. All with our client's product offered as the solution, of course.

To raise this highly relevant communication to the status of hyper-relevance, we added acute timing as well. We used advanced trigger marketing strategies and automated technologies to determine when and how each individual was touched. In this way, we achieved ultra-high relevance, delivering the right message in the right way at the right time. *That's* making an impact.

What's really mind-blowing isn't just that we touch this fifty-something male with the chronic upset stomach on a true one to one marketing basis, it's that we replicate this process across the client's entire customer base, into multiple new segments of consumers and over multiple segmentations of audience demographics and health needs, thereby expanding our customer's reach of its supplement product from seventy-plus only, to appealing to the entire demographic spectrum. This new methodology can do this efficiently and affordably—in real-time with consistency in implementation and repeatability from month-to-month and campaign-to-campaign.

On the next few pages, we'll take a look at some of the outbound marketing messaging generated from the interactive "sticky mechanisms" created to produce genuine relevance and generate consideration across all demographic segments.

Variable Offline Messaging

Adults

Comparison sample A
1 of 36 dynamically generated segmentations in campaign

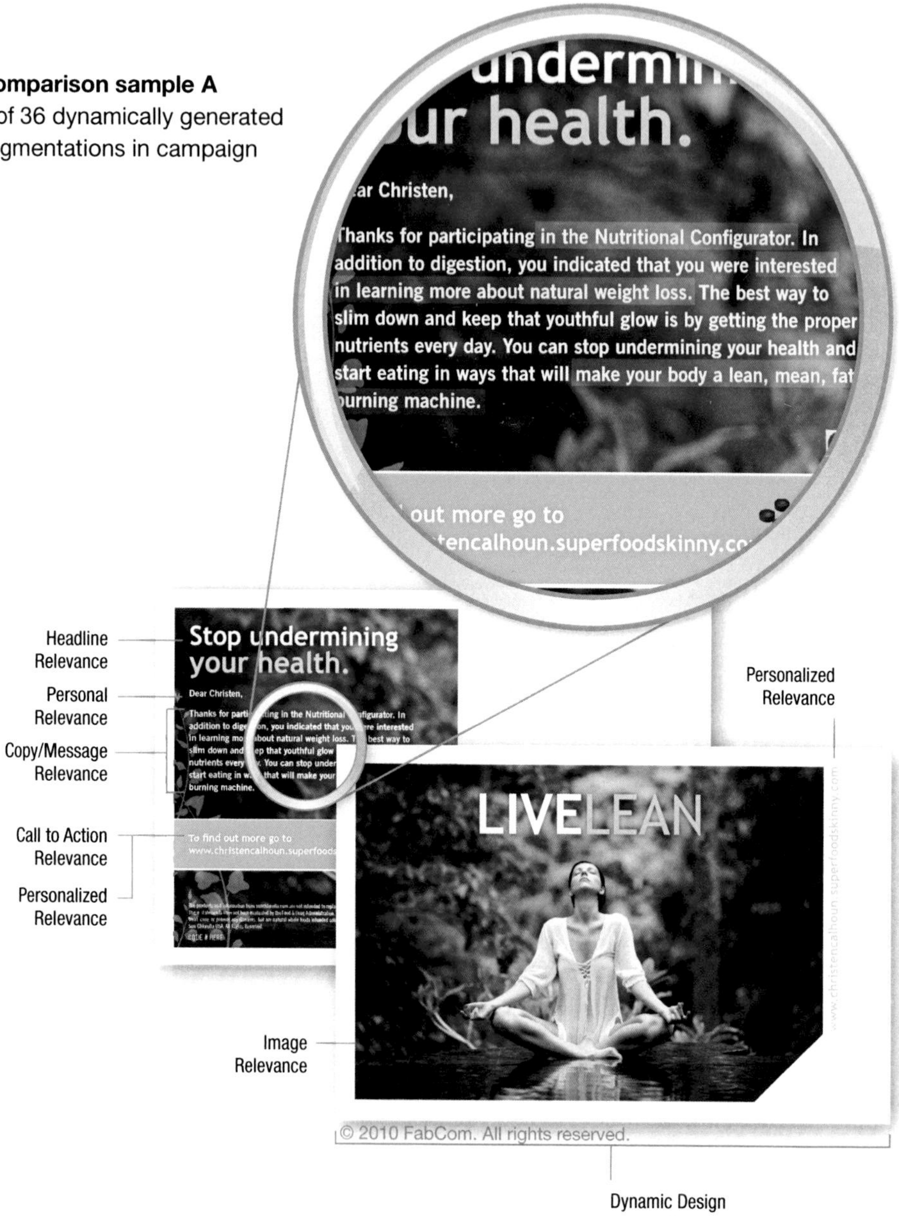

Stop undermining your health.
Dear Christen,
Thanks for participating in the Nutritional Configurator. In addition to digestion, you indicated that you were interested in learning more about natural weight loss. The best way to slim down and keep that youthful glow is by getting the proper nutrients every day. You can stop undermining your health and start eating in ways that will make your body a lean, mean, fat burning machine.
To find out more go to www.christencalhoun.superfoods
LIVELEAN
www.christencalhoun.superfoodskinny.com
Headline Relevance
Personal Relevance
Copy/Message Relevance
Call to Action Relevance
Personalized Relevance
Image Relevance
Personalized Relevance
© 2010 FabCom. All rights reserved.
Dynamic Design

"Sticky Mechanisms" create interactivity to provoke relevance per target.

NOTE: Each element of every communication is customized to demonstrate the product or service attributes that map to that particular potential interest in the brand.

Variable Offline Messaging

Seniors

Comparison sample B

2 of 36 dynamically generated segmentations in campaign

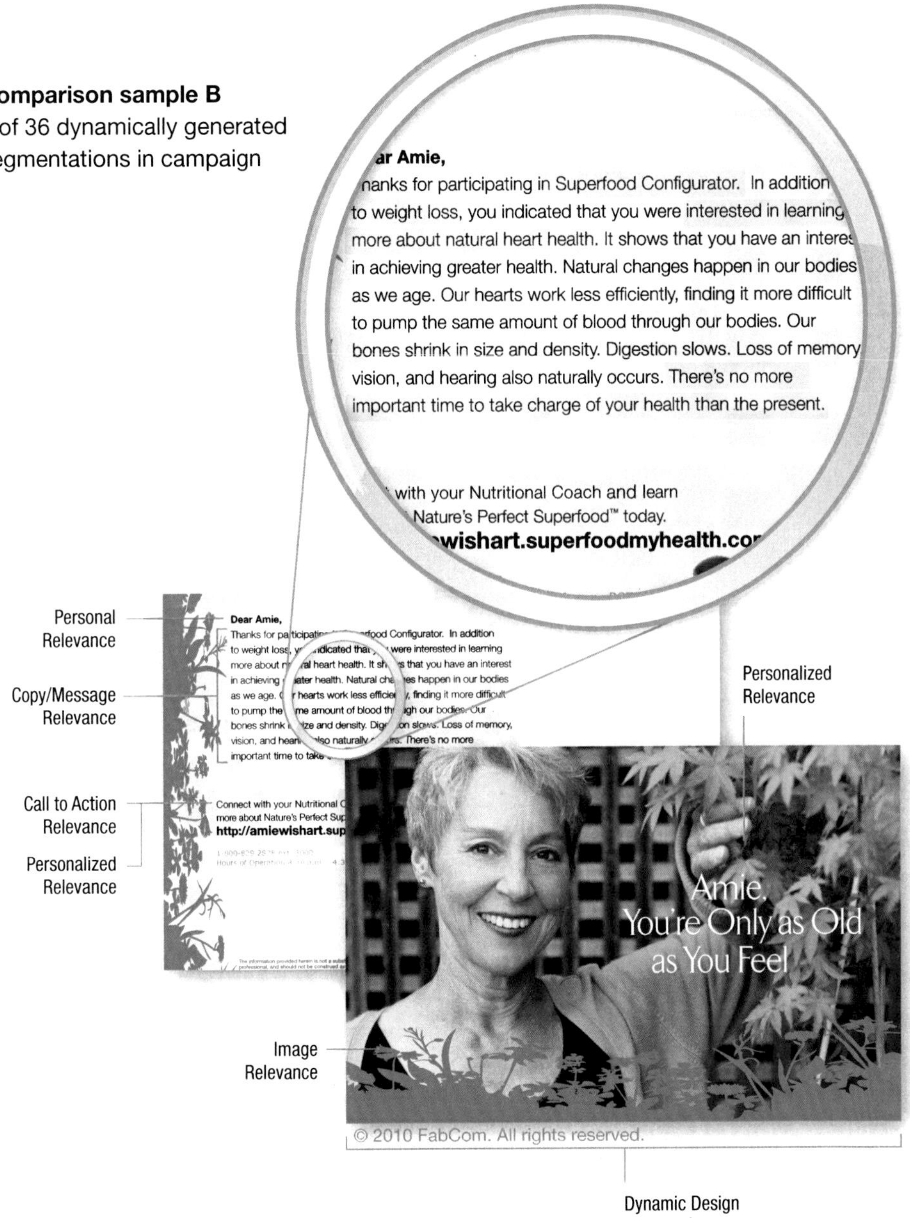

ar Amie,
nanks for participating in Superfood Configurator. In addition
to weight loss, you indicated that you were interested in learning
more about natural heart health. It shows that you have an interes
in achieving greater health. Natural changes happen in our bodies
as we age. Our hearts work less efficiently, finding it more difficult
to pump the same amount of blood through our bodies. Our
bones shrink in size and density. Digestion slows. Loss of memory
vision, and hearing also naturally occurs. There's no more
important time to take charge of your health than the present.
with your Nutritional Coach and learn
Nature's Perfect Superfood™ today.
wishart.superfoodmyhealth.co
Personal Relevance
Copy/Message Relevance
Call to Action Relevance
Personalized Relevance
Dear Amie,
Connect with your Nutritional C
more about Nature's Perfect Sup
http://amiewishart.sup
Personalized Relevance
Amie,
You're Only as Old as You Feel
Image Relevance
© 2010 FabCom. All rights reserved.
Dynamic Design

"Sticky Mechanisms" create interactivity needed to provoke one to one relevance per target.

NOTE: Each element of every communication is customized to demonstrate the product or service attributes that map to the individual's particular potential interest in the brand.

Variable Online Dynamic Messaging

Adults

Online comparison sample A
1 of 36 dynamically generated
segmentations in campaign

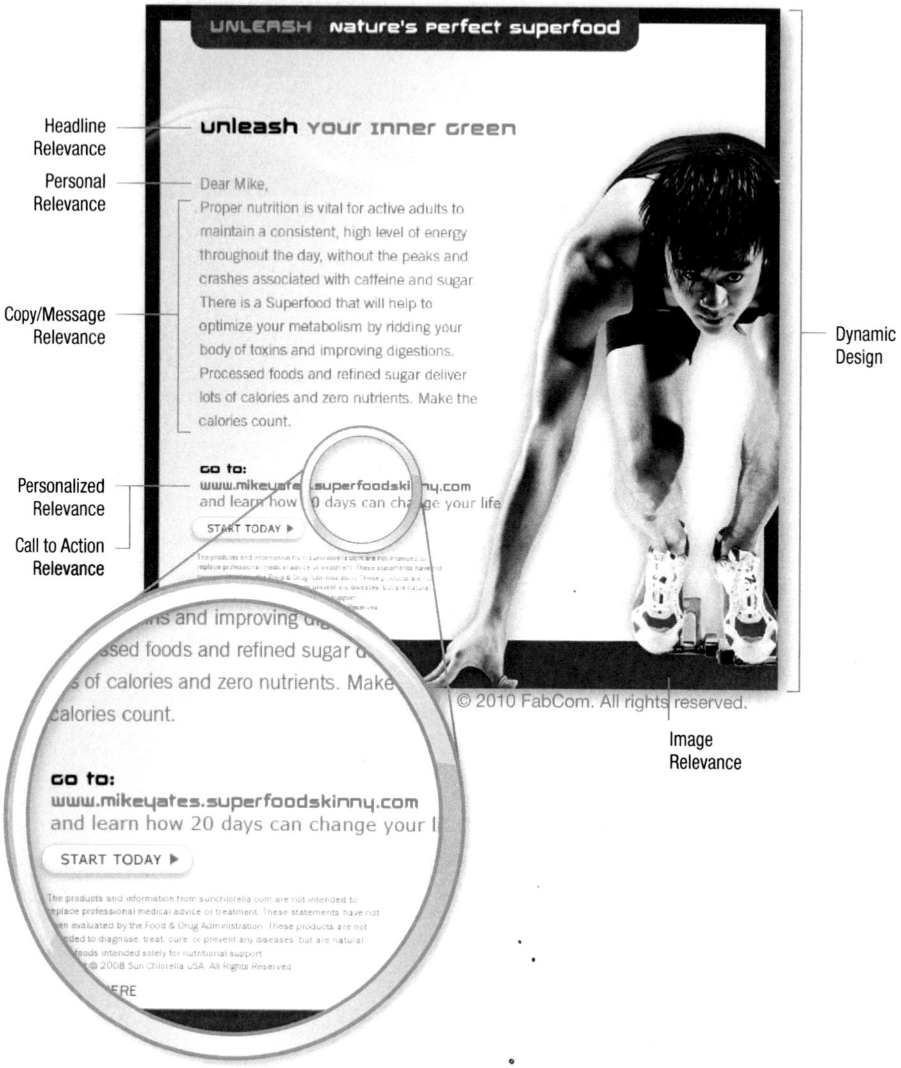

NOTE: Variable information is determined by the customer's past or real-time online or offline interactions with the brand, partners, or competitors.

Variable Online Dynamic Messaging

Boomers

Online comparison sample B
2 of 36 dynamically generated segmentations in campaign

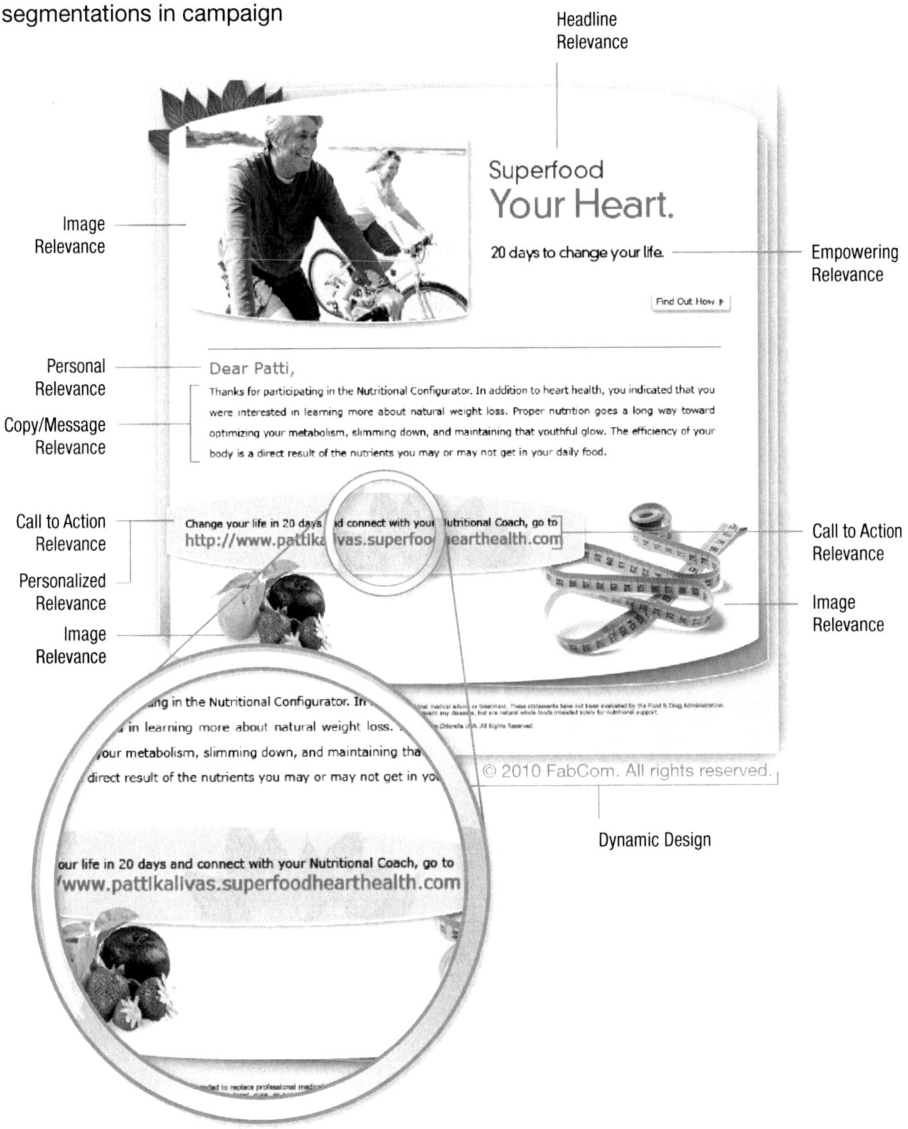
Headline Relevance
Image Relevance
Superfood
Your Heart.
20 days to change your life.
Empowering Relevance
Find Out How
Personal Relevance
Dear Patti,
Copy/Message Relevance
Thanks for participating in the Nutritional Configurator. In addition to heart health, you indicated that you were interested in learning more about natural weight loss. Proper nutrition goes a long way toward optimizing your metabolism, slimming down, and maintaining that youthful glow. The efficiency of your body is a direct result of the nutrients you may or may not get in your daily food.
Call to Action Relevance
Personalized Relevance
Image Relevance
our life in 20 days and connect with your Nutritional Coach, go to
/www.pattikalivas.superfoodhearthealth.com
Call to Action Relevance
Image Relevance
© 2010 FabCom. All rights reserved.
Dynamic Design

NOTE: Variable information is determined by the customer's past or real-time online or offline interactions with the brand, partners, or competitors.

Assembly Required

What does it take to successfully execute such a strategy? Admittedly, it takes a lot of experience and knowledge and just the right technology. You need to gather team leaders with extensive, real-world experience in the various layers of this methodology, from dynamic database marketing to integrated cross-platform technology. You need people at every level of your operation who excel at their part in the process. From writers and creative directors to programmers and brand strategists, the entire team has to understand their role in the implementation process and step up to deliver highly relevant and granular excellence. The bar for marketing professionals is much higher than one to many generic messaging, but so are the returns.

In addition, there is a significant technology investment required. If the old, legacy systems could do this, they would—but they cannot. It takes technology investment dollars and years of experience to get it right the first time. Fortunately, my agency is doing this today and there are a few more leaders emerging across the landscape now. But beware, everyone is saying, "Of course we can do it." The reality is that it takes eight different kinds of programmers, seasoned corporate and marketing strategists, creative directors, art directors, and everyone on the same page; and we mean the *next* page, not the previous page.

You have to think of and create campaigns differently for this opportunity. If we create our new campaigns the same way we do traditional campaigns, they will work the same as traditional campaigns, and in that case, why bother?

For enterprise level organizations, assembling this level of expertise may make excellent strategic and financial sense. For smaller organizations, it may be highly impractical. Better to purchase the marketing services when you need them. For larger organizations, as with anything new and emerging, it sometimes can be next to impossible to reshape from scratch and rethink your entire workflow without the support of others who are accomplished in this area and have already configured practices to sidestep the biggest pitfalls of implementation.

Here's an easy analogy: Building a bike factory to build bikes would not be in most people's best interest; instead, buying the bike from others who already have the factory usually makes more sense. We have deployed these fully integrated cross-channel, dynamic, one to one marketing campaigns for less than $25,000 for some of our smaller customers. We also have other initiatives in the multi-millions that have run for more than two years as of this writing. But, by understanding the opportunity now available, marketers can begin to deploy this methodology, whether through in-house resources or by partnering with carefully-selected strategic partners.

As a result of our investments to date, and other marketing pioneers that are leading the way, smaller companies and brands can now harness the muscle and momentum of the *Google generation* to grow and prosper, rather than be overwhelmed by it. You can break through the inherent barriers of one to many marketing and incrementally increase your marketing ROI by multiplying your brand's reach to include the plethora of one to one marketing pools, rather than simply deploying the old 2 percent strategy and hoping for the best. With this new methodology, media fragmentation and the new emerging channels are no longer a threat to your strategy; they are now invaluable allies you can leverage to deliver improved results more affordably and effectively. That's the power of Neuromarketology.™

In order to fully utilize the power of Neuromarketology™, we must first understand which of the foundational elements of marketing still apply as we plunge into the rapidly changing future of marketing and our ability to leverage the emerging technology.

The principles of branding and positioning continue to anchor successful, efficient marketing, and we'll take a deeper look into those concepts and their application in upcoming chapters. First, we need to gain a clear perspective on the new technological landscape in which we're marketing.

CHAPTER 4—TAKE AWAYS

- Target each marketing channel directly. Provide content, imagery, and messaging that motivates each specific audience at their place and time of choosing.
- Synchronize campaign feeds to deliver the right message, in the right way, in the right place and at the right time.
- Align your company with experienced professionals that have battle-tested the technology and methodology.

CHAPTER 5

Convergence

The technological platform for dynamic, integrated marketing

Technological communications convergence—the merging together of information technologies, networks, and devices—sounds perhaps like some ominous science fiction concept from the future, but it's all around us right now.

Convergence is happening right on your smart phone, iPad, or laptop, which allows you to take and place calls; surf the web; find your location on the planet; play music; receive radio broadcasts; send text messages; take, store, and send photos and videos; and much more to come. Convergence is happening when you pick up your Voice over IP telephone receiver and make a call to your Hong Kong sales associate via Internet instead of on a separate phone line. Most computer networks and the Internet already allow many different devices and operating systems to communicate smoothly with each other by using a variety of intelligent protocols.

Convergence is sneaky; it applies an inevitable pressure that numbs its observers. The sneaky aspect is brought about by its slow and constant pressure that creates the numbness in its students. As practitioners within the areas and/or industries in which convergence is running unbridled, the reactions of leaders must be matched to lag just behind what our mentors taught us was the cutting edge. This sweet spot is midway into early adoption, as depicted by the Technology Adoption Lifecycle curve developed by Geoffrey A. Moore.

Technology Adoption Life Cycle

Geoffrey A. Moore, in his book, *Crossing the Chasm*, describes the Technology Adoption Life Cycle (TALC), which applies to discontinuous innovations such as electronic commerce on the Internet. This innovation is discontinuous because it represents an entirely new way of completing commercial transactions in the marketplace.

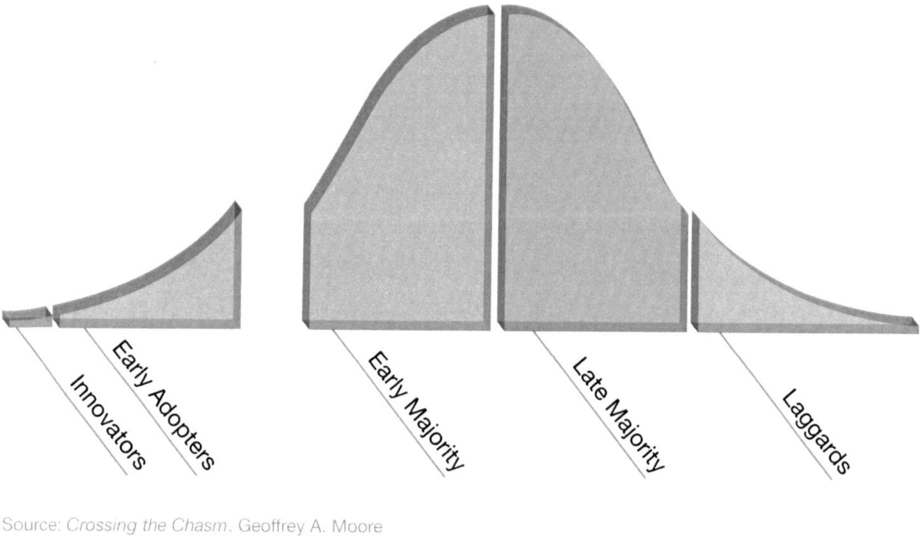

Source: *Crossing the Chasm*. Geoffrey A. Moore

The TALC is represented graphically as six segments on a bell curve. The segments unfold from left to right with the risk-taking innovators on the far left while the risk-averse laggards fall on the far right. In between are the early adopters, early majority, and the late majority.

One aid in observing, monitoring, and projecting the timing and trends of technology adoption is the Gartner Hype Cycle concept, a graphic representation of the maturity, adoption, and business application of specific technologies developed by Gartner, Inc., a leading information technology research and advisory firm.

Gartner Hype Cycle

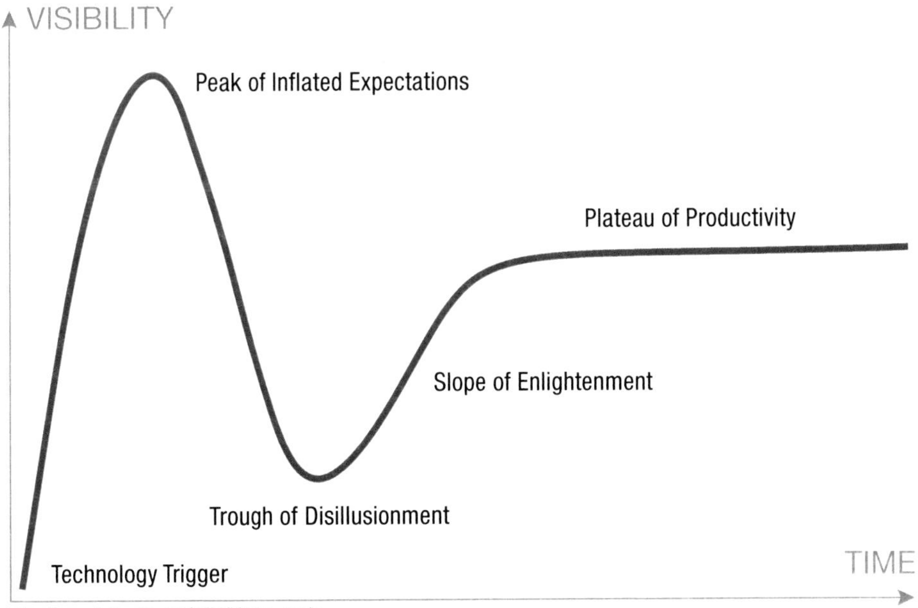

http://en.wikipedia.org/wiki/Hype_cycle

"Hype" is used to characterize the over-enthusiasm and subsequent disappointment that typically happens with the introduction of new technologies. Hype Cycles show how and when technologies move beyond the hype (Peak of

Inflated Expectations), begin to offer tangible practical benefits, and, eventually, become widely accepted. Hype Cycles reflect the scenario we've seen before in technology development and adoption. Something gets hot (media exposure, etc.) before it actually matures, and people become disenchanted with it when it doesn't live up to their inflated expectations. Eventually, the technology is reconsidered (Slope of Enlightenment), and finally, it is applied in a meaningful way and broadly adopted.

In short, the Technology Adoption Lifecycle Curve shows us how technology adoption evolves; the Gartner Hype Cycle adds another dimension to technology life cycle models by attempting to show us why adoption occurs.

If we were to overlay a typical Hype Cycle graph on the Technology Adoption Curve, you can clearly see the sweet spot for adoption.

Technology Adoption / Hype Cycle

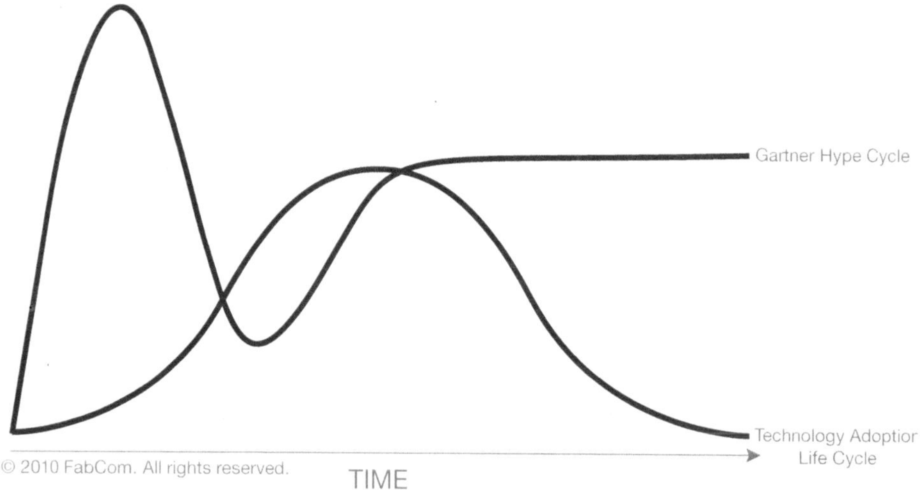

As leaders, we must steward our organization's adoption of new capability profitably. The challenge in matters of convergence comes from many seemingly inconsequential and disconnected progressions that will converge on an industry and accelerate to hyper speeds, not only in reference to capability, but also need, as well as acceptance. We can be pacing along with our techniques to time our entry and, all of a sudden, from the last time we looked, the progression goes from a steady twenty-five miles per hour to one hundred miles per hour.

What's really mind-blowing is that this is only the beginning. I am not exaggerating in the least when I say that, for marketers, convergence over the next few years will have more impact on the way we do business than the invention of the printing press, radio, and television combined.

The whole universe of business will be profoundly impacted. Each industry will be challenged to enable these new and emerging capabilities to reshape not only tactics, but the fundamental strategies that have governed their success for decades. This is especially true in our arena of marketing communications. Those that are the effective adopters, who integrate convergence technology into their core processes, will clearly be the market winners of the twenty-first century. Those who merely deploy new technology to support status quo best practices will be left wondering what hit them.

It's human nature to innovate, but it's also human nature to stay with what has worked in the past. The urgency driving the ideas in this book is that the conditions have *already* shifted, most of us just aren't entirely aware of this. We know things aren't like they used to be; we know the old strategies aren't delivering as they once did. Because what we are looking at is unrecognizable from our past experience; it can be challenging to truly get our bearings.

We are standing at the threshold of an entirely new marketing ecology, a landscape transformed by the seamless and explosive merging of computing, databased information, accessible broadband wireless, and ubiquitous communication network devices. Evolution teaches us that when the conditions change, there are only two options: adapt or become a fossil.

Looking Back, Looking Forward

To gain some perspective on what our horizon actually looks like now, consider the changes we've seen in the last couple of decades. And understand that these changes are not the big show itself, they are merely the prelude, the preliminary foundation for the convergence that is emerging now.

Take email, for example. What business *doesn't* use email today? It would be absurd, unthinkably primitive, to operate without it. We take it completely for granted, yet email only became commercially available in 1993 when America Online and Delphi came online. At that time, there were only a few *hundred* websites! I remember; I was one of AOL's first accounts.

Next came email attachments, and what a revolution that was! Suddenly, we didn't have to walk to a fax machine to send a document or call a courier to deliver art to a client or supplier. It was all accomplished with a few simple key strokes. How did that impact productivity? It put it through the roof. What about client communications and customer intimacy? Suddenly, we could share ideas and reports and any other relevant information via email and a telephone call. It was incredible.

Does anybody remember beepers? Those little black boxes that told you when someone was trying to get ahold of you, and even what their number was? Wow, those sure were efficient ways of getting in touch with people back in the day. Seems like a lifetime ago, doesn't it? Most of us were carrying beepers just a couple decades back and feeling pretty advanced about ourselves. That is, until a little device called a cell phone came into vogue.

Is anybody really questioning whether cell phones will catch on? Of course not, that would be ludicrous. Cell phones are a fact of life. Then why question the bigger picture of convergence, which is where it is all heading?

These are not changes that have happened across generations. These are changes we have seen since most of us began our careers.

Clearly, telecommunications have changed dramatically just within recent memory. That's not the only point of interface between technology and business that has radically altered. Think about how fast data storage has grown. Anybody out there own an iPod or other MP3 player? Of course, who doesn't? Even the entry level models come with more gigabytes than a mainframe had just a few years ago. You can easily get the equivalent of a trunk full of CDs and DVDs, and you've got it literally in the palm of your hand.

But let's think a moment about this nifty device. Does it just make your music more compact and lighter to haul around? No, it's actually a *behavior changer.* Not only can you fit more into far less space, you can *access* it much more easily. Every song is just a fingertip touch away. Let's say you listen to U2 on a regular basis and it's on a favorite list. One morning, on the drive to work, U2 gives way to Led Zeppelin in your heart of hearts, which you haven't listened to it in months. You just do a search by artist, and *click* you've got it.

Now, go back to life before your MP3 player or iPod, to that trunk full of CDs. The first thing you'd have to do if you wanted a different album is pull the car off the road. Can you imagine—you'd actually have to stop driving? Then, you would have to get out and walk around to the trunk, and then start digging. Probably after a couple minutes of this, you'd just say, "Never mind, I need to get to my appointment on time." Or we would not attempt the activity of changing the CD in the first place. We would dismiss the idea as not practical or not worth it. (Remember this "never mind," "not practical," "not worth it," all of it is based on our past experiences that relied on the learned practicalities of a past paradigm.)

Now, extend this analogy to corporate databases, which have mutated in size and accessibility right along with consumer devices. Suddenly, you've got multi-trillion terabyte databases capable of retaining every single customer sigh, whisper, and suggestion of interest, not to mention actual purchase history. Just as importantly, you now have the tools to efficiently access and act on that information.

Remember that "never mind" that came up when it was time to try to dig through all those discs in your trunk? Well, it's no longer relevant. Systems can now deliver up accurate, actionable database groupings in a manner that is so timely, affordable, and effective as to render all objections obsolete.

All this has happened within the span of my teenagers being teens.

Is it that I'm an old man looking back on a glorious one hundred-plus-year career? Not exactly, I've been at it for about twenty-five years. It just so happens that these couple of decades most of us have shared in the business are the ramp up to the greatest acceleration in technology the human species has ever seen. In technological terms, time has sped up. That means we have to keep up to remain relevant, profitable, and leaders in our professions.

The Geeks have Moved on

Technological capability advancements are no longer limited to any one sector of society, such as military or industrial, entertainment or energy, personal or organizational. The transformation is 360 degrees. Take a close look at any aspect of business and society and you will see dramatic change.

We've glanced briefly at the explosive advancement in communications and data storage and management that we ourselves have witnessed. Now, let's give a moment to interactivity.

In 1993, when AOL came online, there were approximately a few hundred websites active worldwide. Now that number is in the hundreds of millions. That's a lot of information and misinformation and everything in between. Again, it's not just about the numbers. The real impact is in the way *behaviors* have changed.

In the Fall of 2001, the dot-com bubble burst and people began re-thinking the Internet. This gave rise to the notion of Web 2.0. Whereas the first generation of web entities were static and supported one-way communications, the new Web 2.0 generation would be two-way, interactive, and dialogic. Blogs, wikis, MySpace, and Facebook were all aspects of the new interactivity.

Remember your organization's first website? It was probably more of a billboard or online brochure than anything else. Now, just a few years later, that would be considered an antique. No longer do we go online just to read. Now, we log on to talk back to, upload and download, to visit and to purchase and borrow and lend, to buy and sell. Does it take a technology expert to make money on eBay or bank online? Hardly. Any American consumer can pretty much pull it off. So, where are the geeks? That's the question you want to ask yourself. Where are the technophiles and true early adopters? When you locate them, you've identified the new leading edge. The geeks have moved on. Sure, they bank online, but that's hardly where their passion lies. The geeks today, the best and the brightest, are on fire with the vision of making the offspring of convergence as common and accessible as Web 2.0.

When did all this happen? When were all these incredible changes not just invented, but rolled out, refined, and woven into the fabric of our daily life to such a degree that we don't even give them a second thought? Probably while we were all busy hashing out that one brand positioning to transcend all others.

We Ain't Seen Nothin' Yet

Here's the power of convergence in action. At our agency, we invested days planning a photo shoot for a client, a high-tech university. We had a full day's work ahead of us with seven sets in nine hours. The first shot was supposed to feature actual students in their dorm watching a 3-D movie and wearing 3-D glasses. We had a full shooting team on hand, including a photographer, art director, lighting and grip, the kind of crew it takes to pull off seven sets in a day and walk away with thirty publishable key images.

We arrive for that first shot and only one student has bothered to make an appearance. The dorm masters who'd helped our staff organize swore that thirty kids had confirmed and they would be there. Kids these days! But, here we were, wasting the client's time and money and no one had shown up for the party. We were at risk of not only losing this shot, but throwing off our schedule for the entire day. Not a good scene.

Here comes the wonder of convergence. That one student who did shows up says, "hold on a minute," pulls out his phone and sends off a text. In less than ten minutes, we've got a room filled with students, who are the perfect diversity mix and motivated by self-selection and their peers, in an instant—we are back on track.

How did we pull that off? By delivering the right message, at the right time, in the right way, to the right people. For example, if we had sent the dorm master out to sweep up some students for the shoot, those kids would have run in the opposite direction. The message had to come from a fellow student.

And it had to be a text—delivered directly to where the students were at that time, and effortlessly forwardable to friends. If texting were not available, we could never have pulled it off. Sure, this student might have sprinted to his computer in his room and sent out an email, but who's to say how many of his peers would have been in front of their screens at that time.

And, clearly the message we used was the right one. The best copywriter in the world couldn't have gotten it better.

This experience really hits home and demonstrates how far we have come. Convergence has been like a snowball gathering speed and mass as it travels downhill. It began in the late 1920s with the inception of AT&T (American Telephone and Telegraph) and has come to dominate the cultural and business landscape in the first decade of the twenty-first century.

Convergence is the force that drives everything we discuss in this book. It drives the explosion of communication channels, output devices, and software/programming capabilities over the past few years.

This convergence of communication technologies and the resulting access also gives us the new, real-time analytical tools and capability to effectively utilize those new channels and new devices to target specific, highly relevant messaging with prospects and customers. In addition, the new technology and resulting new methodology allows a smart marketer to create the personalized connection points and pathways into our brands, which answer the consumers' first and foremost question when considering a brand: "Is this product or service right for me?"

The Accelerating Explosion of Technological Communication Convergence

2010 Neuromarketology™

2006 Twitter 2006 Xbox360 2006 Wii 2006 PS3 2007 iPhone 2008 Dynamic analytics

2001 Cheap computer memory 2001 iTunes 2002 Texting 2003 MySpace 2004 Facebook 2005 YouTube

1999 Broadband 1999 Blogging 2000 Database and trigger marketing 2001 "Smartphone" 20001 iPod

1995 Unified email 1995 IP and Telephony Call Center automation 1997 eBay 1998 Google 1999 Wi Fi

1990 Laptop 1990 Digital photography and video 1990 GPS for consumers 1995 Open source software

1983 Personal computer 1984 Desktop publishing 1985 Windows 1989 World Wide Web

1972 Cable/pay television 1975 Facsimile machine 1977 Mobile phone 1977 Apple computer

1950 Broadcast television 1950 Office copier

1926 Broadcast radio

1876 Telephone

1844 Telegraph

1450 Moveable type printing press

All connect together; create content once, use everywhere (2006–2010)

All work together; create content once, use everywhere (1983–2005)

Each independent; must create unique content for each (1450–1977)

Let's consider, for a moment, the proliferation of video and audio media content over the last twenty years and then compare that to the last ten-year time span.

From Blockbuster to Bust

The first Blockbuster store opened in Dallas, Texas, on October 26, 1985. Brilliant idea! You could affordably rent movies on video tape and watch them at home. No wonder it caught on. Stores started opening around the country on a daily basis. The company became a multi-billion dollar company and was sold to Viacom for a hefty price of $8.4 billion.

But, by the turn of the new century, Blockbuster was losing money in billion dollar increments. What happened? Technology happened. Cable movie channels happened. Bandwidth happened. Netflix happened. Digital downloads happened. Today, its market value and brand is floundering for existence.

This kind of market-rocking progression has happened before, but this time it is happening at warp speed. It will have the same exponential impact as it did the first time it occurred in the 1950s, when television grew out of the convergence of movies and radio. Except this time it's faster, much faster.

Convergence is going on all around us every day, and the pace is clearly accelerating. Communications, information, and entertainment media and channels are morphing and merging on a daily basis to adapt to the furious advances and newfound accountability in technology. Eventually—but not far off in the future—this will lead to a fusion of all channels and media into some single, but as yet unknown, medium—to which you will connect—of course—wirelessly.

As we discuss elsewhere in this book, this convergence of technology provides individuals with a wide variety of convenient ways to communicate—email, telephone, texting, social networking, online, offline as well as on-site and off-site interactions. As individual prospects and customers select the communication styles and platforms they prefer, we, as marketers, have to be able to instantly and relevantly personalize our communications, as well as adjust the placement and timing to the consumer's new preferences and communication points, according to their choices.

More Disruption in the Forecast

A 2010 white paper from IBM on "Building a Smarter Planet" speaks directly to the dramatic changes we see around us now that we must respond to as marketers:

"There's a growing torrent of information from billions of individuals using social media. They are customers, citizens, students, and patients. They are telling us what they think, what they like and want, and what they're witnessing, in real-time. Trillions of digital devices connected through the Internet are producing a vast ocean of data. And all of that information—from the flow of markets to the pulse of societies—can be turned into knowledge, because we now have the computational power and advanced analytics to make sense of it all. That's a lot of data, but data by itself isn't useful. In fact, it can be overwhelming—unless you can extract value from it. And now we can. Everywhere, forward-thinking leaders are achieving near-term ROI. But they are also discovering something deeper. They are finding the hidden treasures buried in their data. We can take the measure of the world's information and actually begin to predict and react to changes in our systems—in real-time."

Clearly, this opens up huge opportunities for businesses, and at the same time, presents huge challenges in terms of the fundamental framework and models of doing business. This business challenge will be further complicated based on the re-convergence of media while our hardware devices diverge and converge randomly per consumer—some users will continue to use, for instance, both a smart phone and a computer, depending upon their physical location and personal lifestyle preferences. We, as marketers, have to be able to respond to those situations to ensure that our messages get through no matter what channel or platform an individual may prefer. That's why experts call this communications convergence a "disruptive" innovation, meaning that it changes a product or service in ways that the experts in the market do not expect or cannot predict—a tectonic shift that disrupts the product and marketing landscape.

Going forward, more and more marketing conversations will take place electronically, but will be powered dynamically. Not only will convergence continue its hypersonic pace, but more and more people will become hooked on using electronic devices as generations mature, offering even more opportunities for connecting with them.

Consider a toddler who walks into the den and sees a Kindle lying next to her father's chair. She walks up to it, points, and says, "Daddy's book." To her, that's what a book is. She may also call printed books "books" as well, but she'll never have to get used to the new concept of an electronic reader—it's already part of her reality paradigm. It's just there, and always has been. If you think today's teens and twenty-somethings are permanently tethered to their electronic devices, just wait until this toddler's generation enters high school.

With technology allowing nearly twenty-four-hour media access as children and teens go about their daily lives, the amount of time young people spend with entertainment media has risen dramatically, according to a study released in 2010 by the Kaiser Family Foundation. As of 2010, 8-18-year-olds devote an average of seven hours and thirty-eight minutes to using entertainment media across a typical day (more than fifty-three hours a week). They spend so much of that time media multi-tasking (using more than one medium at a time), they actually manage to pack a total of ten hours and forty-five minutes worth of media content into those seven and a half hours. The significance? The amount of time spent with media increased by an hour and seventeen minutes a day over five years, from six hours and twenty-one minutes in 2004 to seven hours and thirty-eight minutes today. Due to media multi-tasking, the total amount of media content consumed during that period has increased from eight hours and thirty-three minutes in 2004 to ten hours and forty-five minutes in 2010. This is not evolution. This is exponential and game changing if you are a marketer.

The Case for Convergence as a Catalyst

In the future, everyone from children to the elderly will be thoroughly connected—everywhere, all the time. And because of convergence, every platform, channel, and operating system will integrate seamlessly. From an MRM (Marketing Resource Management) perspective, those of us with the right technology and methodology, the time is already here. We can do it now effectively with an ROI that can take major market share away from competitors who do not possess similar capabilities.

In marketing and business, convergence is key for a number of reasons. First, marketers have learned that they must put the customer at the center of their universe. In this customer-centric universe, marketers must respond to the customer's preferences in communication, and every communication must be relevant to the individual recipient—in timing, place, and message. Secondly, convergence nurtures business growth by creating economic synergies that reduce the cost of communicating and convergence creates new value models. A simple old school/new school example: rather than placing an expensive newspaper ad to reach target audiences, marketers can send an online communication at a much lower incremental cost.

Convergent devices and content *now can* also integrate with customer relationship management applications to communicate more effectively and efficiently, while at the same time gathering, storing, and analyzing huge amounts of data about individuals, their preferences, and their detailed interactions with a company. We can use the large amounts of collected data—*now* in real-time without the traditional hassles of acquisition, mining, cleaning, and purposing—to help ensure that every customer and prospect communication is highly personalized and relevant to the recipient. This not only adds relevant impact and ROI to every marketing communication, it also has a positive effect on customer relations as well.

Call Centers have been so impacted by convergence, we call them "Contact Centers." Through the rise of the Internet and its transition to mobile devices, social networks, and increasing globalization, Contact Centers must now deploy capabilities across many channels and platforms—not just phone calls. In fact, there has been a tremendous shift in doing business from phone calls to the Internet. Nearly 80 percent of all retail brokerage trades are now made online. This expansion of capabilities may contribute to the outsourcing of U.S. contact center functions to foreign countries—you can't hear a foreign accent in an email.

Advancing computer capabilities and networks are also allowing us to converge the information systems in businesses. Instead of marketing, operations, customer service, and accounting all operating independently and often on different and incompatible platforms, we can now *link* all these functions together to share and benefit from the continuous flow of real-time data and communications. The marketing department can know immediately when a customer makes a purchase and can automatically generate a follow-up communication for customer service and add-on sales. Customer service has, for years, had a complete and real-time current record of a customer's activity on everything from initial purchase to billing and payment patterns. Now, with convergence, we can deploy it seamlessly to the front lines of our marketing battles.

Convergence is much more than just the evolutionary development of technology. It is a force that alters the relationships and playing field for businesses, consumers, media, and the marketplace. It changes how information and entertainment are provided to consumers and businesses and how the recipients process and utilize that information. Because of the rapid explosion of new media channels and platforms, we are now living in a world where media literally surrounds us every day. Technological convergence has already created a converged culture.

The Converged Culture

As a result of technology and communication convergence, we are also seeing a convergence of the governmental and regulatory bodies that control and monitor the networks and devices. As the walls between what were once completely separate services come tumbling down in convergence—data, video, voice—regulators are challenged to redefine their overview and market perceptions.

Ray Kurzweil, author of *The Singularity is Near: When Humans Transcend Biology*, and other futurist thinkers have popularized the concept, similar to and growing out of technological and communication convergence, called "singularity," which they see coming in our near future. Singularity is when a self-improving artificial intelligence develops beyond the capability of human intelligence—when the machines know more than we do. On the leading edge of marketing technology and methodology, we've already reached a singularity of sorts—the machines cannot only know and retain more information about a customer than a live salesperson ever could, the system can use that information to automatically generate a unique, transparently personalized, relevant in real-time, communication for that customer and deliver it to them on any communication platform they use—from the mailbox to the iPhone.

Because of convergence, advertisers, advertising professionals, and media content suppliers must completely re-think the traditional way of doing business. Customers and prospects demand a personally-relevant, interactive relationship where they can be involved in the creation and modification of messaging, not one in which they simply receive information. We must also converge the traditional methodologies we have employed for creating marketing messages. To hold the interest of customers and prospects in our new tech world, we must change the way we talk to them. Not only do we have to provide a dialogue, but we must also incorporate elements of both branding and direct response in our messaging, which, in the past, had always been kept separate.

The simple theme throughout this book that links together all of the disparate areas that must be coordinated to deploy Neuromarketology™ is that **marketing is no longer about publishing to your customers and prospects; it is about creating a dialogue with them** that works on *their* specific terms.

CHAPTER 5—TAKE AWAYS

- You as a marketing leader must either adapt as the conditions change or fall behind.
- When you harness the convergence of communication technologies and the resulting marketing possibilities, you will be provided with new tools and capability for one to one dynamic marketing.
- The whole universe of business is being profoundly impacted by convergence. Marketing evolution and automation has been occurring on an increasing rate over the last decade as the component parts have been introduced. You still have the right timing to adopt before mainstream acceptance. Keep going, keep learning, and do not let go of the vision of higher returns from each marketing dollar invested.
- Don't leave the tech to the techies. It is imperative that you as a marketing leader understand the ins and outs of the technology so you can use that knowledge to build your new processes that are supported and connected by the glue of technology and innovative thinking.
- Convergence and the new capability save monthly resources. Use the efficiency gained when you harness the new capability of convergence by repurposing the savings into reaching one more segmentation.
- When thinking of our converging cultures, think about individuals becoming their own personal rendition of Spiderman, casting webs of communication and creating connections to your messages.

- The masses are dictating how and when convergence must evolve. This opens wide doors of opportunity to provide multiple channels of communication into your company. Walk through the door.

- Customers are the most important part of the marketing process; configure your marketing based on what *they* want, not based on what you can do now.

- Assign one team member to provide a report about a converging area that could affect your marketing in the future. Have this report presented at a normally scheduled monthly meeting to ensure you are educating your team.

CHAPTER 6

Positioning Revisited

From Trout and Ries to today

With so much happening technologically, it's critical to emphasize that these advancements do not replace sound marketing strategy or impactful creative. Rather, they inform and update those strategies and resulting tactics to render them more relevant than ever in a contemporary context.

To truly understand the place of strategy and creative excellence, we must look at where we have been and see where we are going. The modern age of marketing began in the spring of 1972 when Jack Trout and Al Ries published a series of articles in *Advertising Age* magazine, titled "The Positioning Era." Their subsequent landmark publications, *Positioning: The Battle for Your Mind* and *The 22 Immutable Laws of Marketing*, established them as thought leaders in a field that had previously relied on direct response, price/feature advertising fueled by creative hunches, slogans, jingles, and the advent of television for its successes. These books have become more than "the bible" of marketing. To a seasoned marketer, Trout and Ries' books are more like the stone tablets Moses brought down from Mount Sinai—the very foundation of modern marketing. These books are the first body of work to provide thoughtful, fact-based, actionable guidance on meeting the challenges of communicating to an over-communicated society.

Until the early 1970s, some marketers talked in general terms about perhaps creating an image for their product. Most commonly in those days, when advertising agencies talked about image advertising, they were trying to placate a customer when an ad ran and nothing happened to improve sales. "Oh yeah, that was an *image* ad, not a selling ad."

Trout and Ries were the first to present a specific strategy and tactics for positioning a product into one of the few available slots in the prospect's/customer's mind. Once you own that prime mental real estate, you have a brand. They were the first to articulate, in concrete terms, the power of creating an emotional connection with your customers that engenders unswerving loyalty and defies logic.

I repeat. They articulated that positioning is not something you do to your product. It's something that happens in the mind of your customer. By presenting a strategy-driven, consistent position in everything you do for your target audiences, you earn preference over your competitors. Your communications become believable. Your position makes a specific promise to prospects and customers. If their every experience with your product fulfills and demonstrates that promise, with carefully-crafted messaging, every experience can be positive or negative, but whichever it is, it establishes your brand. Even the local mom and pop pizza shop can be branded as the best or most authentic neighborhood pizzeria.

How Does Branding Happen?

Let's play a word association game. Quick—without looking at the words below, cover them with your hand. Then uncover one word at a time. When you see each word, say the first company name that occurs to you.

- Soup
- Ketchup
- Cola
- Coffee
- Athletic shoes
- G-rated movies
- Tires
- Overnight Delivery
- Jeans
- Rental Cars
- Ivy League College
- TV Viewer Research

I'm willing to bet that you said Campbell's, Disney, Heinz, Levi's, Nielsen, Nike, and Starbucks. Hundreds of other people, from all walks of life, industries, and cultures, have had the same reaction when I played this game with them. Some categories may have a couple of players in your mind—for example, Goodyear or Firestone for tires—which is not as good as owning a category all by yourself, but it's better than no awareness at all. Each of those companies reached each of those consumers for different reasons and accomplished something remarkable that pays ongoing equity to its stakeholders.

How did Disney and Starbucks and the others earn their prominent place in your mind? It's a pretty extraordinary thing, when a brand is so strongly entrenched in our culture that I can predict your automatic response upon seeing the product category. So, how does that brain branding take place?

It's not cheap, although once established, a brand will repay your company many times over what it costs to develop. It's not a magic wand or silver bullet—no matter what some practitioners of the advertising craft would like you to believe. It didn't happen just because of a catchy tagline or a memorable jingle. Nike didn't become *Nike* simply due to Michael Jordan and Tiger Woods wearing swooshes at every appearance.

A brand burns its way into our brains via all of these tactics and many more. It's a range of many factors that lock a brand into our consciousness. More precisely, it's the communication of the factors that get a prospect to consider the message and, ultimately, to *try* a product. When the product, service, or message lives up to its promise in the buyers' experience, *that's* when branding happens. Branding ensures repeat purchases. The brand becomes a habit and serves as a shortcut in the purchase decision process.

It's the cumulative effect of consistently experiencing a myriad of factors that brands your customers' and prospects' brains. The following illustration shows a few of the elements that combine to create the branding experience in the brains of customers and prospects.

Neuromarketology Drivers

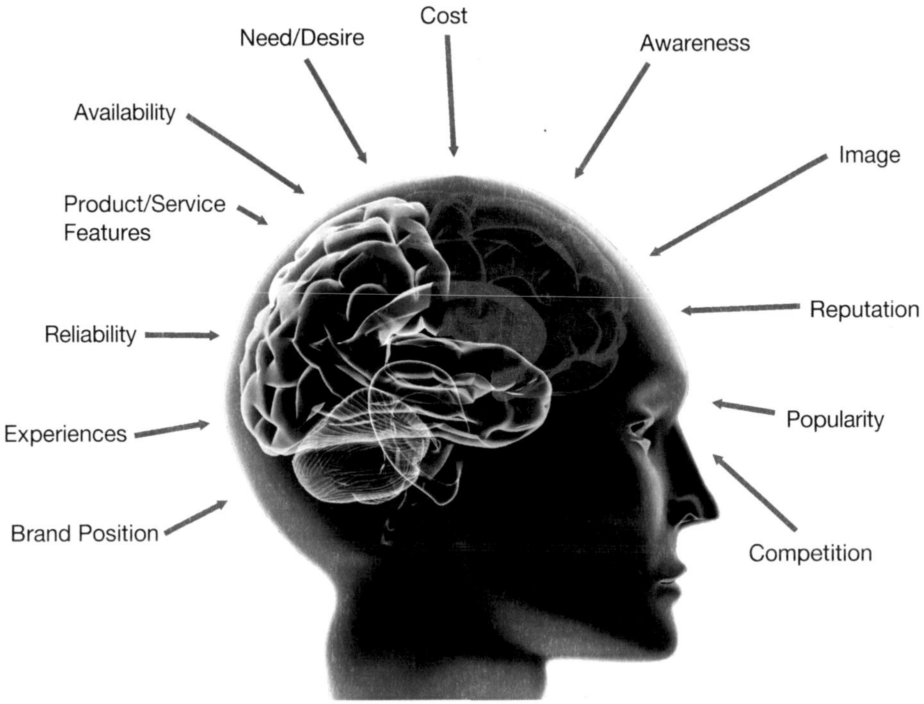

The above illustration includes just a few of the infinite considerations that burn a brand into the customer's brain. The nuance is to understand each of these consideration criteria are all utilized by every consumer as their top criterion at different points in the buyer's progression. Even when we do a great job, the final decision on everything we do as marketers to gain the benefits of branding is eventually made in a place we can't control: the *mind* of the customer/prospect.

The Mind of the Marketplace

We can examine, study, and—to some degree—influence what goes on in there. Ultimately, as Trout and Ries first articulated forty years ago, marketing wars boil down to a battle for the minds of an audience.

When it comes to branding, what *you* think is important and appealing about your product doesn't really matter. What matters is what the *audience* thinks is important and appealing. Your brand can only become what the market audience allows it to be. You have to find a "hole" in your market, a time and place where audiences are not getting what they want from competing products. Then, you position your product as the solution that fills that hole.

Here's a quick example from the frozen food market of finding and filling the hole in a category. As you know, there's a lot of frozen food out there.

At the time, Stouffers was known as the *best* frozen food, the gourmet frozen food.

When it got crowded in the gourmet food category, along came Lean Cuisine. They created a new category in the mind, one they can be best at: *low calorie* gourmet food. (Hence the word cuisine.)

So now the mind has a place for frozen food (probably occupied by Kraft), gourmet frozen food, diet gourmet frozen food. What's left?

How about low priced gourmet frozen food? Ever heard of Budget Gourmet? Now, we could obsess about whether this is really an "against" positioning strategy because it's a contrast to the high priced Stouffers, but the point is that when we say best, we're not talking about being the best in the galaxy and dominating the universe. Not even best on the planet, the country, or the state.

In this example, we observe that there's a hole in the market between premium and lower price. How do you fill it? Budget Gourmet brand frozen meals! This fills the hole between budget and gourmet food lines.

The essence of positioning is to accept prospect/customer perceptions as your reality and then restructure those perceptions into dynamic, emotionally-resonating messaging that maps to your brand attributes to create the position you want in the market. The better key audiences understand a brand's promise, the more effectively the brand is differentiated from its competitors.

What's a Brand Worth?

An established brand is a valuable corporate asset—for a company, its investors, and its employees. Of all the things a company can own, an established brand is far and away the most important.

Founders die. Offices burn down. Machinery wears out. Interest rates change. Technology becomes obsolete. But, with proper nurturing, the brand endures. Brand loyalty is the only sound foundation on which business leaders can build enduring, profitable growth.

If your marketing is effective and persistent, prospects and customers are going to remember one thing about your product, no more. The one thing they should remember is your position—what your product stands for, the promise it makes to the market. Don't challenge them to try to remember more than one thing; you will lose that battle for the mind and therefore lose the marketing opportunity.

Positioning Poker—You Only Have Five Cards to Work With

The study of the human brain has recently resulted in a number of insights—many of which you'll hear more about in later chapters. But one of the earliest marketing/brain revelations was that there are only five basic positions that can be effectively and reliably occupied in the mind (AKA readily believable). Only five positions consistently make sense to the human mind when evaluating choices in a market. The five positions are shown on the left in the chart below that also includes examples of products that have benefited from successful positioning.

POSITION	PRODUCT	POSITIONING STATEMENT
Best	Hertz	We're #1
Niche	Apple Computer	Think Differently
First	Levi's	The Genuine Article
Against (Contrast)	7-Up	The Un-Cola
Combination	FedEx	When it absolutely, positively has to be there overnight (example of First + Against)

Once you've done a deep analysis, including quantitative and qualitative research combined with the experience of knowing how to connect the dots from the research, and determined the position that makes sense for your product in its specific circumstances, you must implement the positioning so that it is unique, credible, meaningful, actionable, strategically correct, adaptable, defensible, and sensitive to environmental forces.

Let's take a look at how the battle for the customer's mind looks in one category. This is called a Mind Space Map.

Mind Space

Rental Car Category

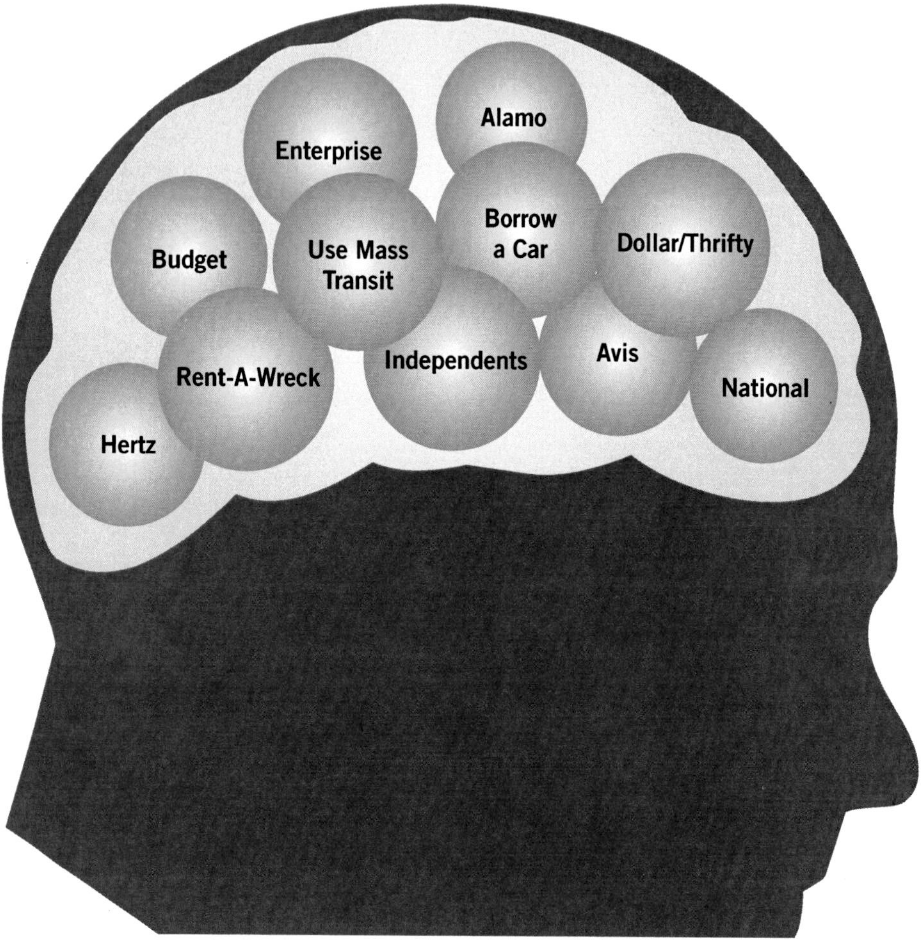

Notice that eight out of these eleven are positioning on some version of "against high prices." That's the definition of cut-throat competition.

Bewitched by the Possibilities

In the 1970s, the concepts of positioning and branding began to change the way we thought about marketing and more predictably delivered sought-after results. That wasn't yet the case in sit-com ad agencies. I was about seven years old and *Bewitched* was one of my favorite TV programs. The husband of the star worked at an advertising agency. The day-to-day life of account executive Darrin Stevens at the McCann-Tate advertising agency seemed exciting, creative, and critical to the world of commerce. Even when there were problems, the big idea saved everyone's job and always seemed to make the clients happy by the end of the show. I remember one day turning to my mother and telling her, "That's what I want to be when I grow up—a Darrin Stevens."

That was a fictional account in a simpler time, when advertising for most companies and advertising agencies was a matter of a big idea and just buying some TV spots, a smattering of print ads, and maybe some direct mail. But, you still had to get the message and target audience right in order to establish a product's position successfully.

Trout and Ries' *20th Anniversary Edition of Positioning: The Battle for Your Mind* updated their thoughts and concepts regarding positioning and marketing, mostly in terms of the playing field they re-visited at the very beginning of the twenty-first century. Much has changed in the world of marketing in the decade since their updated book. The Immutable Laws and their guidance on positioning still hold up just fine in terms of strategy. It's just that the whole game of marketing communications has become much more complicated and challenging by the plethora of media outlets, splintering of target audiences, new communications platforms, and, let's face it, more competitors all claiming the same thing in the same way.

Marketing has never been a breeze—we're dealing with the individual reactions and perceptions of human beings, remember. Marketing may not be nuclear physics, but in many ways Einstein had it easy. He was dealing with infinite numbers of atoms, which all behave similarly and predictably under the same set of circumstances. In marketing, we deal with infinite numbers of individual human minds that are, as you'll agree, mostly unpredictable. Even within a single demographic profile and given the same circumstances, the human mind can vary dramatically from one individual to another.

In addition, there are a few other challenges that make marketing today more difficult than ever before. It's more fraught with the perils of goals unmet and money wasted than it was even just a few years ago. There used to be six major outlets for messaging (a one-in-six chance of getting it right). We now have fifty-plus options to place our messages (a one-in-fifty chance of getting it right the first time). Then, we must divide by approach, messaging style, message, etc. You can clearly see that without professional guidance, advertisers face hundreds of permutations and options that splinter the chance of getting it right the first time, down to the same odds of winning at craps.

It's a Whole New World . . . Every Couple of Years

In the ten years since the publication of the updated edition of Positioning, the alternatives for delivering marketing communications have exploded. Television, once the most dominant and often only consideration when it came to media selection, is today simply one choice among many. Over the past decade, the impact of innovations in personal communication options on the planning, creating, and implementing of marketing initiatives has grown exponentially and is accelerating. When it comes to devices and/or media that can address large audiences, it's as though the phenomenon of television is being introduced every couple of years.

New ways to access huge audiences are actually being created at a faster pace than most marketers and agencies have been able to keep up with—email, text, integrated communication devices, PDAs, PURLs, social marketing (blogging, Digg, Facebook, Twitter), cloud and proximity networks, and messaging. When these many opportunities present themselves so fast, a lot of them are missed and, just as crippling, a lot of money is wasted chasing the wrong ones.

There is also an ever-rising level of competition and a lowering of the bar to communicate, adding to the marketing and media clutter that make marketing today more difficult than it's ever been.

We can summarize the challenges of the current marketing environment as follows:

- Trying to predict the perceptions and reactions of unpredictable human minds.
- Geometrically increasing number of media platforms to reach large audiences.

- Rapidly expanding competition and marketing clutter in every product and service category.
- A long-established lack of accountability and foggy models on marketing ROI.

Do these major challenges crush any hope of ever reducing the risks of marketing, let alone getting the results you need to grow your company profitably?

No. You can learn how to break down and overcome what seem like insurmountable challenges and how to avoid gambling on personnel or suppliers that can't get the job done.

The first key to success is understanding that, even amidst these challenges, successful marketing still comes down to a core ability to communicate and connect with:

1. The Right Audience with
2. The Right Message with
3. The Right Timing in
4. The Right Place.

We'll describe how to combine the science of Neuromarketology™ (the study of marketing's effect on the mind) with advanced technology and strategic thinking to help you accomplish all of these fundamental tasks, ask the right questions, create projectable marketing success, and know exactly whether and how your marketing is paying off incrementally, the way it must to achieve your goals.

Now that we've reviewed just how difficult predicting marketing outcomes can be these days, let's take a look at recent breakthroughs in neurology—brain science—that can help make the job of communicating effectively and efficiently with prospects/customers more straightforward and less susceptible to the winds of chance. We took a peek inside the brain in this chapter with the topic of the five basic positions; in the next chapter we'll go even deeper to find the answers you need.

CHAPTER 6—TAKE AWAYS

- Positioning is not something that you do to your product; it is something that happens in the mind of the customer as a result of proper branding, positioning, and ongoing marketing efforts.
- Build your brand messaging around what your audience thinks is important and appealing, *not* what you or your boss thinks.

CHAPTER 7

Brain-Branded

The biology of one to one marketing

In my youth, one of the intern jobs I took to break into the business was working on the Pepsi Challenge, the well-known taste test marketing campaign that Pepsi started in 1975 and is still used to this day. I was the guy sitting in the supermarket offering customers two tiny paper cups, each exactly half-filled with either Pepsi or Coke, and asking, after they tasted the blind samples, "Which did you like better?" Because I wanted to be in advertising and received intern credit, it was a great job. (Even though I was, and still am, a Coke over Pepsi kind of guy.) I felt like I was already in advertising. The Pepsi Challenge also taught me a lesson about marketing that was one of the most important I ever learned.

In those days, Coke significantly outsold Pepsi nationally, due in some measure to Coke's forward-thinking strategy focusing on agreements to supply outlets such as restaurants and vending machines. In searching for some marketing leverage against the better-selling and more widely distributed soda, Pepsi came up with the Challenge. Pepsi quickly discovered that, in this taste-test format, more people chose Pepsi over Coke consistently. Videos of consumers choosing Pepsi over Coke soon became the feature of Pepsi's TV ads (I still believe Pepsi missed a huge opportunity by not using one of the tests I conducted in a TV spot).

While Coke continued to have the larger market share, Pepsi made clear gains in market share with the Challenge campaign. That's the reason Pepsi was careful to say in their ads, people "prefer the *taste* of Pepsi over Coke." People bought more Coke than Pepsi, but Pepsi consistently won the taste test.

Pepsi Challenge

Old School "one to one marketing"

It was an eye-opening experience for me. Whenever I lifted up the privacy cards and showed a "Coke person" that they had chosen Pepsi, or vice versa, many would get very agitated and accuse me of any underhanded trick they could think of. "You switched the cans." "You made one colder than the other one." "Oh you're wrong, I always drink Coke."

Of course, I hadn't cheated; we had very strict rules about keeping everything exactly the same for the comparison. Participants simply refused to believe that their senses had failed them. They held on to their firm belief in their life-long beverage of choice. The realization of the awesome power of marketing, the very idea that advertising could ultimately have the power to make someone a life-long true *believer* in something, even when their own experience tells them differently, is what finally convinced me that I had to be in this field. At that point, I didn't actually know what a brand was, but I began to understand what it could do.

Let's back up for a minute. If more people in the national marketplace chose to drink Coke, why did Pepsi consistently win the Challenge in the local supermarket? In his book *Blink*, Malcolm Gladwell offered one answer: in a taste comparison, based on a small sip of each product, more people will choose the sweeter taste; Pepsi is sweeter than Coke. When drinking in normal quantities over the long term, more people prefer a less sweet taste, so more Coke gets sold each year.

A few years ago, a neuroscientist recreated the blind taste-test Pepsi Challenge in his lab at Baylor College of Medicine. He placed his test subjects in an MRI machine and monitored their brain activity while they compared sips of Coke and Pepsi. The findings confirmed the results of the original

Pepsi Challenge, the region of the brain thought to deal with feelings of reward responded more strongly to Pepsi than to Coke.

The neuroscientist, Read Montague, PhD, then ran a second test with one difference. For the second test, Montague told his subjects beforehand which sample was Coke. The results changed dramatically; almost all second test subjects claimed they preferred Coke. Furthermore, in the second test, the medial prefrontal cortex of subjects, the area of the brain thought to handle high-level judgment and reasoning, showed a response to the Coke sample. (Don't worry; we'll sort out the function of key brain regions and their relation to marketing later in this chapter.)

In the second test, subjects were thinking about their choice of beverage in a different, deeper, more complex way. It wasn't simply, "Oooh, sweet . . . I like." More evaluation was going on in this non-blind test than was the case in Montague's first blind test.

When researchers reversed the protocol for the second test and told subjects which cup contained Pepsi, the results didn't change—Coke was still the preferred choice in the non-blind version of the Challenge.

The Power of Brand Over Matter

So, what accounts for the strong preference for Coke when subjects know they're drinking it? It's the brand. People were evaluating the Coke sample in their minds in a much deeper way, connecting it to their perceptions and memories of Coke over the years, not just making a simple taste judgment. They were thinking about "The Real Thing" positioning; they were thinking about the lovely portraits of Santa, illustrated by Haddon Sundblom for decades of Coke holiday print ads. They may even have been envisioning themselves standing with hundreds of others on a seaside bluff, with the wind blowing in their hair, singing, "I'd like to buy the world a Coke. . ." or "I'd like to teach the world to sing. . ." When they knew they were drinking Coke, the test subjects reacted based on the full range of their past experiences with Coke's brand, positioning, and its ads, not just the taste of that small beverage sample in their hands.

The Coke brand is a beautiful thing; after all these years its power is demonstrated every day around the world. In the U.S., the Coke brand is a revered cultural and marketing icon that has led the soft drink market for over a century and a quarter, actually dominating its market for much of that time. Pepsi got a later start, stumbled along the way, and spent a lot of money on radio and print ads from the 1930s into the early '50s to position itself as the low price alternative to Coke, the market leader:

"Pepsi-Cola hits the spot.
Twelve full ounces, that's a lot
Twice as much for a nickel, too
Pepsi-Cola is the drink for you."

Catchy jingle, but the positioning of lower price is obviously not as engaging as Coke's more evocative positioning. The Pepsi brand and its positioning have simply never grabbed the national imagination the way the Coke brand did and has never established the same emotional connection with consumers that Coke has earned and enjoyed over the years. Now that's great marketing!

"Emotional connection? I thought we were talking about science and the brain?"

Well, it turns out that, when it comes to responding to products and their marketing and advertising, our brains are about as rational as a family reunion. In other words, emotion rules the day. It's only in the past few years that the leading researchers such as Dr. Montague, in the neuroscience labs, have provided real evidence of the role that emotion plays in our purchase decisions.

Before we take a look at more of these neuroscience research findings, let's pop the hood on the human brain and see how the various parts go together and what type of thinking they do in terms of responding to product and marketing stimuli and establishing perceptions.

The average adult human brain weighs about three pounds and has a consistency similar to tofu (and don't we all know people who think as though their brains are tofu?). The brain consists of three distinct layers, each with a different type of cellular structure and function.

The outside layer—the cerebral cortex—***is the folded, convoluted, "gray matter" with which we're all familiar. It is the most recent part of the brain to evolve in humans and plays the key role in:***

- receiving and processing input from the senses (sight, taste, hearing, smell, touch, and balance)
- selecting and implementing voluntary movements
- organizing sensory information for coherent perceptions about the environment, abstract thinking, and language

The cerebral cortex is where the brain *thinks*. For years it was thought that economic decisions and perceptions were controlled only by the frontal cortex, the rational, thinking brain. Recent neuroscience studies have proven this to be only partially true. Longer-term financial or economic rewards are evaluated in the rational mind. But the benefit of immediate rewards—like taking advantage of the "2-for-1" sale when you only need one right now—are controlled by the second major area of the brain, the limbic system, where emotions are processed. So, in the context of a sales pitch, or any other marketing communication, emotions come first.

The middle part of the brain—the limbic system—***evolved next after the cortex and was the first brain region that could process*** emotion and feelings. In an evolutionary sense, this brain development was necessary for survival because mammals give birth to live young. Mammal parents needed to love and care for their offspring and this required feelings.

Finally, deep inside the brain, sitting on top of the brain stem is the "first," "old," "lower," or "reptilian" brain, ***which focuses on basic*** survival functioning such as breathing and blood circulation. When a patient in a coma is pronounced brain dead, that is, has no conscious thought, this part of the brain continues to function. The reptilian brain (essentially the same structure as a snake's brain, although obviously much different in size) is responsible for triggering decisions—***such as "fight or flight"—based on the information processing of the cortex and limbic system.***

So, for the purposes of leveraging marketing communications, those are the three major regions of the human brain: cerebral cortex, limbic system, and the reptilian brain. Brain research related to Neuromarketology™ today also focuses on three smaller structures that researchers have identified as pleasure centers:

Nucleus accumbens
A set of brain structures, part of the limbic system, associated with sexual arousal and the anticipation of pleasure or reward. That's why sex sells.

Medial prefrontal cortex
A region within the cerebral cortex that plays a role in planning complex thought processing, personality expression, and moderating behavior for social acceptability. Here is where customers make the final decision to buy—"I want it. I'm going to do it."

Insula
This structure, also within the cerebral cortex, is associated with emotions, anticipating pain, perception, motivation, addiction, and interpersonal experience. This area of the brain activates when a potential customer anticipates a possible problem with the purchase—high price, for example. Much as the medial prefrontal cortex makes the decision to buy, the insula can negate a purchase decision.

That's a quick overview of what happens where in the human brain, at least in terms of our interest in how it reacts to marketing communication. Here's an illustration to summarize these structures and their respective areas of influence in your marketing efforts.

The Biology of Decision-making

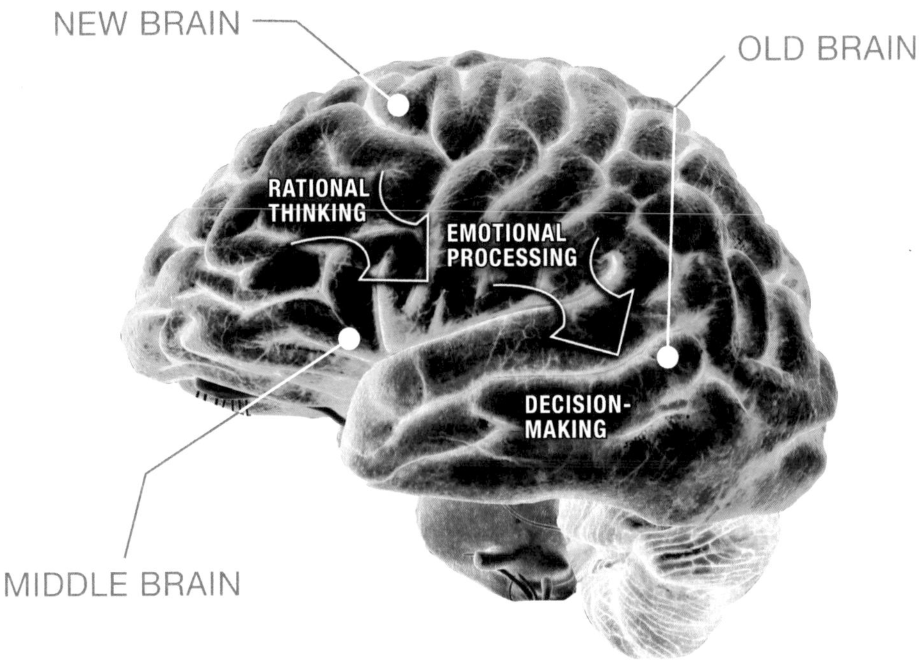

Mirror Neurons

One of the first neuroscience studies to have direct implications for marketers took place at the University of Parma in Italy, one of the oldest universities in the world. Beginning in the 1980s, neuroscientist Giacomo Rizzolatti and several colleagues were conducting an experiment in which they placed electrodes through the skull and into an area of the cortex of monkeys' brains to study individual neurons, or nerve cells, that are associated with the control of hand and mouth movements. For example, some neurons were active when a monkey grasped a peanut and other neurons fired when the monkey put the peanut in its mouth.

One day, while preparing to run another trial in the experiment, a researcher had a monkey's brain electrodes plugged into the recording device and, when the researcher reached for a peanut to hand it to the monkey, the monkey observed the researcher and the monkey's neurons fired just as though the monkey itself had reached for the peanut. This remarkable and lucky observation led to a breakthrough in neuroscience leading to the discovery of "mirror neurons."

Eventually, Rizzolatti determined that approximately 10 percent of the neurons in a monkey's cortex have mirror properties and fire similarly in response to both performed hand actions and observed actions. Recently, evidence from functional neuroimaging (fMRI, which is discussed below) and behavioral studies strongly suggest the presence of similar mirror neuron systems in humans, which respond during both action and the observation of action. The mirror responses in humans have been shown to come from the same brain regions as those observed in Rizzolatti's monkeys.

Mirror neurons are why, when I watch my son racing to the other end of the basketball court for a breakaway lay-up, my heart races as though I am running, too. The mirror neurons in my brain are telling me that I'm also driving for that lay-up. Mirror neurons are also why, when my son comes down awkwardly on an ankle, I wince in pain. They are also the reason that we feel good when someone smiles at us and we automatically smile back.

In his 2008 book, *Buyology* (which I recommend highly), Martin Lindstrom tells a story about Apple's Steve Jobs to illustrate the impact of mirror neurons on product and marketing dynamics. One day in 2004, Jobs was walking down Madison Avenue in New York City and he realized that a significant number of people he passed were wearing the distinctive white ear buds of his recently launched iPod. Jobs is quoted as saying, "Oh, my God, it's starting to happen." Mirror neurons, triggered by the sight of the new, cool earbuds worn by other people, were telling consumers, "You need that now to be cool," and consumers were responding by getting their own iPods. Mirror neurons are the driver behind any fad or successful product launch. We see something, we imagine ourselves having it. In anticipation of that reward, our mirror neurons cause dopamine to be released in the nucleus accumbens and prefrontal cortex, that makes us feel good and so, we buy or commit. Yes, it's a *thought* process, but a thought process based in emotion and provoked by on-target marketing that drives the anticipation of reward.

How do the neuroscientists get inside our brain to determine how and why we respond to products and their marketing? Scientific and medical ethics preclude implanting electrodes into human brains simply to figure out why the iPod is so popular (for now). But fortunately, for those of us marketers truly attempting to refine our craft, there are several non-invasive technologies that can give us insight into brain functioning as it relates to marketing.

Buying and the Brain

Electroencephalography (EEG, thankfully) is the recording and analysis of *electrical activity* in the brain as captured by sensors placed on the scalp and head. It is sometimes referred to as "Quantitative EEG" or QEEG. Subjects can be asked questions and shown products or images of products, while the changing electrical activity in the brain can be isolated to specific brain regions. EEG's limitation is that it can really only measure electrical activity in the outermost layers of the cortex. EEG's advantage over other methods is that it is instant reading as compared to resolution times of seconds or minutes for other methods. It is also less expensive than MRI technology.

Magnetic Resonance Imaging, specifically a specialized form known as functional MRI (fMRI), measures brain activity by graphically reporting the dynamics of blood flow within the brain. This test is performed in the widely available, but still very expensive, piece of lab equipment in the shape of a large tube into which the subject slides. Again, the subject can be asked questions or shown various items and the technology records and displays the brain activity. As mentioned above, the measurement of blood flow is slower than measuring electrical impulses, but fMRI is more accurate in indicating *where* in the brain the activity is taking place.

Another older technology, eye tracking, may also be used either by itself or in conjunction with either EEG or fMRI. A lab device follows and records where the subject is fixing his or her gaze over a period of time while observing a product or advertisement. Correlating the eye tracking data with other data on brain activity can, if assimilated properly, lead to insights regarding packaging or marketing communications messaging.

In terms of specific, directly-applicable guidance for more effective, more efficient marketing, neuroscience is by no means a perfect science today. This new information can certainly help us in reducing the risk of off-target marketing and advertising, but it is only one data point among many that we need to master in order to better communicate with prospects and customers. The emerging findings in this field must be used in conjunction with other quantitative and qualitative research data in order to provide a more complete picture of who we're selling to and what they want. When we add all these components together and then analyze our options through the magnification and granularity of these new data points, we form the nucleus of Neuromarketology™.

One big advantage that neuroscience brings to marketing is that we no longer have to rely solely on focus groups and surveys to gather data about how customers and prospects think about products and marketing. Focus groups and surveys are notorious for being skewed by cognitive bias, which is a technical research term meaning people lie. It's human nature to want to look good and look smart, so most people will say what they think will achieve that objective in a focus group or on a survey. Neuroscience allows us to see what's happening subconsciously in the brain of the subjects before they have a chance to fluff it up a little to satisfy their egos.

Neuromarketology™ studies, to date, have proven conclusively that marketing involves a high degree of emotion and is not an entirely rational process. Here is the one simple truth about every great marketing campaign: You must get a person emotionally involved in your product or message. Remember, it's the limbic system that deals with emotions in the brain. Only when there is an emotional connection between your brand, product or message, and your target, will the limbic system bump the final decision up to the cortex with a strong recommendation to move forward.

We're not completely controlled by perceptions, but perceptions definitely inform our decisions, and perceptions are formed unconsciously in the brain. Perceptions of branded products are the result of a complex, subconscious process that results in our conscious, rational mind deciding we have a good reason to like something and/or to purchase it. The art and science of great marketing is harnessing those points of connection and franchising those connections with your brand efficiently and with measurable consistency.

In the next chapter, we'll look at the wealth of other defining research data we can apply, along with brain science, to better understand, communicate with, and meet the expectations of target audiences.

CHAPTER 7—TAKE AWAYS

- When marketing is done properly, alignment between messaging, timing, and the target audience can influence someone to be a lifelong, true believer.

- Establishing a relative emotional connection with your customers and prospects is essential in effective advertising and brand building.

- We can accomplish an emotional connection by understanding the demographics, psychographics, and behaviors of our targets and creating the messaging to align their emotional reactions with the investment into our products or services.

- This alignment is a perfect balance of messaging authentically and simultaneously to all three levels of the brain:

  —The cerebral

  —The limbic

  —The reptilian

- We no longer must rely on what looks good or what we think might work. Using the science of Neuromarketology, you *can* map out quantitatively what will have the highest percentage chance to provide the intended results.

CHAPTER 8

Raising the Relevance

Next level audience research and segmentation

Not everything that counts can be counted, and not everything that can be counted counts.

Sign in Albert Einstein's Princeton office

The wisdom is knowing the difference.

Brian Fabiano

In the last chapter, we explored brain science and its value as one point of data in planning and creating more effective marketing communications. In this chapter, we'll look at the other points of research data that we can correlate with Neuromarketology™ insights to deliver dramatically improved return on investment. As one of the many sets of research data that can be helpful in marketing, perhaps the discussion of Neuromarketology™ could have just as easily fit in this chapter. However, I felt that since much of the neurological data related to marketing is relatively new and not yet widely understood, a separate chapter was warranted.

The point of effective marketing research is to more precisely and efficiently *segment* your target audiences so that your media selection and messaging can be personalized as individually and intimately as possible. This book's main message is **as we go about segmentation, enable your brand to function like the facets of a diamond (see illustration on page 14), by mapping *all* of your brand attributes directly to all of the profitable segments**. Do not segment out your growth markets due to conventional wisdom that does not take into account the new technology, new methodology, and exploding communication channels that allow you to now include those groups and their resulting sales.

Effective, efficient marketing communication requires knowing *where* to find the target audiences, *how* to speak to them, *what* to speak about, and then *when* to reach them (message timing). "Where do they congregate so I can communicate with as many as possible at a relatively low cost?" "What are their hot buttons likely to be for a particular type of opportunity?" "Would they rather receive an email or a direct mail piece or a message on Facebook?" In addition to defining primary audiences, we need to identify and engage our target audiences' secondary influencers and communicate effectively with them in a manner that leads them to help move your potential audiences to action.

For instance, a college targeting high school students for enrollment must also deliver its brand message to the students' parents, their peer group, and influencers such as teachers and counselors. When this is accomplished with sequential and dynamically controlled content, it is efficient as well as effective.

Market segmentation is the study and categorization of target audiences into subgroups of individuals or organizations sharing one or more characteristics, beliefs, or values that cause them to have similar needs and expectations and require a unique communications approach. A true market segment meets all of the following criteria:

- it is meaningfully distinct from other segments,
- it is homogeneous within the segment (all members share common attributes, attitudes, needs, and/or expectations; also referred to as a cohort),
- the majority of members respond similarly to a market stimulus, and
- members can be addressed by marketing initiatives.

The segmentation process itself consists of segment identification, segment characterization, segment evaluation, and target segment selection. If each segment is primarily homogeneous in its needs and attitudes, members of the segment are likely to respond similarly to a given product, marketing strategy, method, or vehicle for marketing communication. That is, they are likely to have similar feelings and reactions to a marketing mix for a given product, sold at a given price, and distributed and promoted in a certain way.

Effective market segmentation requires steely objectivity and significant experience to clearly derive target audiences' real needs and desires without allowing any personal cognitive or organizational bias to color those observations and analysis.

By applying a variety of data and methodologies, we can refine the characterization of segments in a way that is actionable, meaningful, and guarantees influential communication.

Intelligent analysis and market segmentation can significantly improve the effectiveness of marketing communications. With intelligent, accurate segmentation, communication can be optimized, the right target audiences can be defined, advertising results can be improved, and customer satisfaction can be increased.

In times only recently past, it was enough to segment your target audiences and differentiate your marketing communications simply based on the target audiences' age range and the similarities in needs, desires, and perspectives that each age range cohort shared. That's no longer the case.

As with everything else about marketing, audience segmentation has become more complex. The challenge is not just a function of the rise of the Internet. People have become more individualistic and more diverse in their interests and perceptions from generation to generation. Just as the media options have fractured and multiplied today, so have the needs and personalities of consumers. We can no longer use age-based demographic segmentation alone to craft persuasive marketing messages and predict how the target audience will respond. Demographics are now just *one* of the multiple and divergent points of information we use to compile and segment target audiences.

The familiar categories (described on page 121), served marketers well for years as shorthand for knowing the when, what, how, and why of communicating persuasively with each broad segment. Some generalizations can still be made for each segment and are noted, but *only* if you integrate this information with other personally-relevant data of behavior, psychographics, and environment in order to make segmentation and messaging decisions.

Technological convergence directly impacts all aspects of marketing. But, when it comes to relevancy of communication, an entirely new dimension is added to the equation. Previously, targeting revolved around what we might call the message/audience axis. Craft the right message for the right audience, and you're on target. Of course, this strategic and creative output needed to be supported by the right media buy. *Oprah* for women. *Monday Night Football* for men. Obviously, this is a gross over-simplification, but compared to the media explosion we are undergoing now, it isn't. In fact, media delivery opportunities have become so varied and so personalized, that they require us to rethink what audience relevancy really means today.

Matching the right audience with the right message is great, but if you stop there, you've just missed the twenty-first century. The new dimension of marketing relevancy is the timing/behavior axis. Traditionally, advertisers such as Ford didn't buy spots on *Monday Night Football* just because that was the ideal time to get men thinking about the purchase of a new truck. It's just where the men were hanging out. The timing element was simply folded into the message/audience axis. In effect, the right time to reach men was any time you could reach them, whether those guys were looking for a new car, interested in trucks, or focused solely on football and guacamole.

This brings us to the matter of behavior. The behavior advertisers were targeting was their audience's viewing behavior (or listening behavior, in the case of radio; or reading behavior, in the case of print), not their buying behavior. It was relevant enough to know that the men most likely to buy the F-150 were most likely to watch *Monday Night Football*, compared to other shows.

What if you could know when those members of the *Monday Night*

Football watching universe had actually visited a dealership or did a little window shopping online? Furthermore, that they had hit the truck pages. We know that guys love to check out vehicles even when they're not buying them; what if you could tell when a *Monday-Night-Football*-watching, truck-loving male of the species had visited those truck pages several times within a week, indicating heightened interest, and perhaps could pair that information with visits to a credit union site for car loan research? Then you sent them your new truck messaging. Now, that's taking relevancy to the next level by achieving ideal timing triggered by actual behavior. This is the new dimension of marketing relevancy that technological convergence supports.

Data mining companies are already negotiating partnerships with high traffic sites to purchase behavioral information from their users and aggregate it across the Internet. This "intent data" can be used by marketers to target for demographic, geographic, lifestyle, and purchasing patterns. The availability of such intent data will make ultra-high relevancy a standard bench mark for high performing organizations in marketing.

Let's say you're a resort in Vail, Colorado. It's great to know that families enjoy your atmosphere and price point. But, how much more useful would it be to also know of people shopping for flight information to Denver during ski season? What better time to reach out to those people with a special offer than when they are actually planning their ski vacation? This offer could arrive by way of a carefully crafted online contact. Or it could be promoted in the form of advertising purchased and placed specifically because of this information. In this way, this ultra-high, time-sensitive relevancy can generate far greater value in media purchasing.

Already, agencies and marketers can use intent data to define a standard audience, then track them across any online ad network or portal. This information allows us to not only drive campaign choices, but also to track success, or lack thereof. Wouldn't it be nice to know if you're off-target before you've committed a full quarter's media spend?

Traditional "Age and Era" Population Segmentation

The GI Generation **born 1905-1924**

Formerly, this was a key consuming generation—responsible for the post-war blossoming of the American consumer market. Today, these seniors have their consumption limited mainly to health care, assisted living, and funerals. The segment is shrinking dramatically in numbers as well. This segment can also be targeted through their Boomer children/caregivers. They still respond to late night TV ads, especially with an age-appropriate spokesperson.

The Silent Generation **born 1925-1944**

This is the smallest generational segment in numbers; these seniors are now mid-sixties to mid-eighties. Their consuming days are mostly behind them. As a group, their lifestyle reality means they respond to messages including "maintain your independence," "delay aging," "paid by Medicare," and "stay in your own house." They love a deal and can be reached through traditional print and broadcast media, especially newspapers. They are happy coupon clippers.

Boomers **born 1945-1964**

Seventy-five million strong and consuming with a vengeance, the Baby Boomers are now retiring at a rate of about one every eight seconds. They have been proven to respond to messages of convenience—make their lives easy and save them time. Value is also important to Boomers so, "no rip-offs, man." While good numbers of them have transitioned in one degree or another to the Internet, they can still be reached as well with conventional print and broadcast media. The biggest Boomer marketing success reflecting these trends? Viagra.

Generation X **born 1965-1984**

This segment can never consume at Boomer-like levels because there are nine million fewer of them. Gen X favors cyberspace over traditional media. The Internet's breadth and fragmentation makes them a challenge to reach. Examples of top Gen X product successes? The iPod, iPhone, iPad, and the i-whatever-Apple-says-is-the-next-cool-thing. The folks at Apple aren't just talented technologists; they're also branding experts at creating and defining what's cool for this generation segment in particular.

Generation Y **born 1985-1995**

There are ninety million of them consuming at a rate of 500 percent of that of their Boomer parents. It's the first generation to routinely have brand new cars in high school parking lots and conduct much of their social life online. They are highly fickle consumers—fashion styles can barely keep up with them. They look for "green" companies and those that have a good humanitarian record in dealing with workers. The principal media for reaching them is cyberspace, but again, fragmentation can make online contact tricky. Oddly, they do respond to direct mail and anything that is personalized for them.

Generation Z **born 1996-present**

Also known as "Generation Next" and the "iGeneration," these are the true "digital natives," having been online and otherwise connected their entire lives. This cohort's oldest representatives are only about fifteen years old as I write this book, so it's difficult to speculate about their characteristics because not as much is firmly established about their characteristics or behaviors compared to the other cohorts.

Latinos, Approximately Twenty through Forty Years Old

Fifteen to twenty million strong, this geographically-defined market is here to stay. A valuable market segment, especially at the supermarket. They can be targeted with conventional Spanish language or mainstream media, but just translating a promotion from English to Spanish is often a deadly mistake—if you're going to use Spanish language media, create the content in culturally-appropriate Spanish.

The Rest of the Story

In today's markets, we are finding on an increasing level that it is no longer good enough to plan and execute marketing communications based simply on broad age and era cohort similarities in beliefs, values, and expectations. We must dig deeper.

Without more information, how can you explain or respond to the fact that, for example, two forty-five year olds, who appear demographically identical, can have diametrically opposed perceptions and expectations on many issues and products.

This conundrum, and our ability to solve it, has been a powerful new business development point with potential new clients for our agency for years. On the next page is a sample ad from our agency that we placed in the local *Phoenix Business Journal* across from the list of top advertising agencies. It was selected as the top ad in the book. The ad size is 10"x13" so shrinking it to display in this book is challenging, but you can take a look at it in full size by going to www.fabcomlive.com/businessjournalad.

Fortunately, we now can use psychographic, behavioral, and sociographic data to supplement information about broad demographic segments in order to better plan and target marketing communications. In addition, we can analyze and account for environmental and other external factors that may affect communication with a particular target audience, such as transaction, behavioral, and trigger-based messaging. By further segmenting the broad traditional age-based demographic categories, we can begin to craft our messaging more effectively by analyzing and understanding social status, group interaction, and buying habits.

FabCom Business Journal Ad

They're both 40-year-old college graduates, yet you can't talk to them the same way. We can help your marketing resonate with your audiences, no matter how diverse. We analyze the demographic, psychographic and behavioral segmentation of your target audiences to create messages that precisely influence their perceptions and reactions. Our team then deploys the power drawn from the convergence of business, marketing and creative strategies to develop high-impact marketing that increases your ROI. It may seem like mind reading, but there's a wealth of solid science behind our proven capabilities. Do you need to reach more of your best prospects?
Go to www.showmethecustomers.com
fabcom
www.fabcomlive.com

Headline Reads: They're both 40-year-old college graduates, yet you can't talk to them the same way.

This type of analysis allows us to think of individuals in a target audience segment in very concrete terms and in great detail. By combining the various types of research data available to us with consumers' environmental and behavioral information and their real-time progression in the buying cycle, we can know a lot about each of the members of the segment: what turns them on, what turns them off, what messaging catches their attention, what holds their attention, what makes them tune out, what they have been searching for or buying in the last few days or hours, and what brings them to the next level in the buying sequence. In short, with good, objective research data from a variety of sources and solid experience in analyzing and applying that research, along with the deployment of dynamic marketing funnels, we can know, with confidence, how, when, and where to communicate persuasively and engagingly with any segment of the target audience.

After demographic segmentation—only the very tip of the starting point in an accurate segmentation formula—the next step in focusing on your target audience is psychographic segmentation—sorting an audience segment along more behavioral lines related to attitudes, interests, needs, wants, values, beliefs, personality, or lifestyle. You've already read about the fracturing diversity of target audiences in the marketplace; psychographic variables help smart marketers take into account the cultural implications of this diversity and use that information as a tool to further refine the messaging and the reach to our audiences.

In my organization, we use a modified version of the "VALS" psychographic profiling model, which can filter a demographically segmented audience or group of audiences in seven dimensions as detailed below. This additional layer of information can make messaging much more effective and efficient because we have a stronger sense of who we're talking to. VALS is an acronym for "values and lifestyle" and was developed at the Stanford Research Institute.

Seven Psychographic Profiles (VALS)

BELONGER

This largest group makes up about 40 percent of the population. They are "the average person, in the average town, in the Midwest." They love community and being with family and friends. They frequently drive U.S.-made pickup trucks or large U.S.-made sedans. They are very nationalistic and don't like change. Their best time is spending time with their friends, talking, having fun, and hanging out. They are hard working, extremely conservative in their views, and most likely religious. They will often buy because of personal relationships, so you need to take the time to get to know them. Belongers are very brand loyal.

ACHIEVER

The Achiever is a group of about 5-7 percent of the population. This is the serious businessperson who is constantly looking to become more and to make more. Power and physical wealth is the major stimulator that makes this person perform day in and day out. This individual is likely to drive a Lexus, BMW, Mercedes,

Porsche, or other high-end luxury car. In contrast to the Belonger, these people need to be individuals, to set themselves apart from the rest. They will always buy the top-of-the-line and the latest in technology. Achievers control about 90-95 percent of the money in the U.S. If you want to effectively talk to Achievers, make sure you make it quick, and make sure your message talks about individuality, about innovation, and most of all, about power, money, and profit.

EMULATOR

Emulators make up about 15 percent of the population. Everyone in this group would love to be an Achiever, but isn't. The emulator will try to do anything to make him or herself look like an Achiever with the goal of attracting the opposite sex or the approval of peers. They will buy the flashy, but lower-end foreign imports or domestic copies because they can't afford true luxury. It might be the top rap artist, the top movie actor, the top sports star they are trying to copy, not the businessman. This group suffers from low self esteem, needs peer approval, is usually under thirty years old, frequently not financially stable, but will spend whatever money they have on anything that will make them look like their ideal: successful. If you want to talk to Emulators effectively, you need to make sure that whatever you are trying to sell them will make them seem just like the person they are emulating: the successful Achiever.

SOCIALLY CONSCIOUS TYPE A

The Socially Conscious psychographic group is comprised of two types. Type A is about 20 percent of the population and Type B is about 7 percent. Type A is concerned with the effects their actions have on society as a whole. They want to make the world a better place. They are environmentally concerned, they recycle, they buy things that are environmentally friendly, and drive fuel-efficient cars. They believe in schooling and teaching children and are frequently highly educated, mostly in the liberal arts. They like to help the homeless and the poor, the socially disadvantaged. Slightly conflicted, they are quite cynical about society and its flaws, yet take a generally positive view of how the future could be. You must sell something that is making a positive difference to either society or the environment. Being educated, these people can quickly see through fake environmentalism and social conscience.

SOCIALLY CONSCIOUS TYPE B

Very much like their cousins in Type A, most of the generalizations of Type A will apply to Type B, except that while Type A believes that there is hope for humanity as a whole, Type B has given up on humanity as a whole, and has moved off into their own small communities where they live socially conscious lives within their socially conscious group. One can find these little islands spread all around the country, not only in the hippie communes in California, but also those that have sequestered themselves away in the hills of Montana, religious communities in Texas, and communes that can be found all over the country that don't believe in personal property. These people are mostly self sufficient, and purposely cut themselves off from the world, so they are unlikely to be open to marketing offerings.

BALANCED / TOTALLY INTEGRATED

The Balanced segment is the smallest of all the groups, accounting for only 1-2 percent of the population. The Balanced group is basically a mixture of the Achiever and Socially Conscious types. You might say these are Achievers with a Social Conscience. There are many examples of people who have grown rich, who have achieved power and wealth, but still are concerned to ensure that their rewards don't come at the expense of society, rather with the cooperation, and to the benefit of, humanity and nature as a whole. For the most part, they are too busy to listen to you unless you have something of specific interest to offer them. They will do their research before seeing you or will have the staff do so.

NEEDS DRIVEN

This final segment consists of about 12 percent of the population. These are people who buy on impulse and instinct, depending on what they need at the time. Even if on a budget, they will often pay more because, instead of doing the weekly shopping trip to the supermarket where things are cheaper, they will buy things last minute at the corner store. Another curious thing about this group is that they will frequently flash money around. In this way, there is a bit of emulator there, but they are not trying to emulate anyone in particular, they only want to prove that they have money.

In addition to this VALS-modeled data on attitudes, expectations, and behaviors, smart marketers turn to a litany of other research databases that segment the consumer and business markets into more precise behavioral groupings.

External/Environmental Factors

Once we have determined the demographic and psychographic segmentation of target audiences, we overlay any environmental or other external variables that may impact the audience segments' perceptions, expectations, and reactions. A dynamic marketer must look at both geographic and sociographic variables to fine-tune the understanding of the audiences and optimize communication with them. Among the factors we consider are:

Geographic variables

- Region of the World or Country: East, West, South, North, Central, coastal, hilly, etc.
- Country Size: Metropolitan Cities, Small Cities, Towns
- Density of Area: Urban, Semi-Urban, Rural
- Climate: Hot, Cold, Humid, Arid, Rainy

Sociographic variables

- Gender
- Family Size
- Family Life Cycle
- Socioeconomic Status
- Religion
- Nationality/Race
- Language
- Brand Loyalty
- Product End Use
- Readiness-to-Buy Stage
- Decision Making Unit

In addition to the demographics, psychographics, and sociographics of an audience, we also need to look at what we call the "customer lifecycle." By determining where a prospect or customer may currently be in terms of their consideration and purchase relationship to a product or brand, we get an even stronger indication of what they need and want to hear, as well as how to communicate it most effectively and deliver the message most efficiently. The four phases of the customer lifecycle are: Awareness, Consideration, Purchase, and Loyalty. The addition of the industry's recent breakthroughs in dynamic information sharing across media channels and departments with the right kind of marketing resource management platform also lets us know, in real-time, information such as: what the targets have been purchasing at a store online or offline; what their interactions are with the contact center; what they have been searching; what content they have been clicking on; what pages they are taking the time to view; and which features/attributes of your brand, product, service, or experience you offer that the customer does not care about.

The graphic below shows how prospects and customers move through their evolving relationship with a product or brand—from hearing about it for the first time to becoming a long-term customer. We'll look at this lifecycle more closely in the chapter on one to one integrated micro-marketing.

Customer Lifecycle

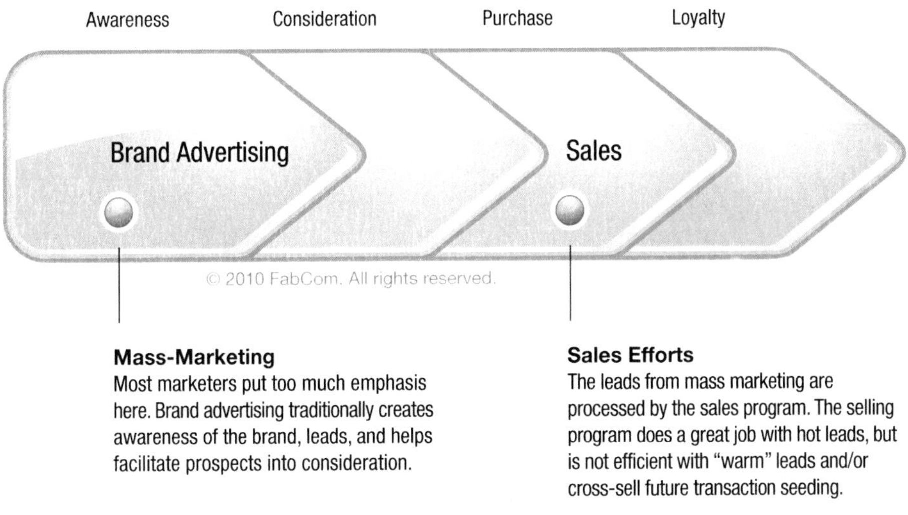

Awareness
Consideration
Purchase
Loyalty
Brand Advertising
Sales
© 2010 FabCom. All rights reserved.
Mass-Marketing
Most marketers put too much emphasis here. Brand advertising traditionally creates awareness of the brand, leads, and helps facilitate prospects into consideration.
Sales Efforts
The leads from mass marketing are processed by the sales program. The selling program does a great job with hot leads, but is not efficient with "warm" leads and/or cross-sell future transaction seeding.

But Don't Stop Here . . .

A smart marketer does not stop gathering and analyzing data until they're convinced they have exhausted the resources available. At our firm, we are constantly speaking with, and analyzing the motives and buying behavior of, consumers and business decision makers and seeking out additional reliable sources of information. A great deal of our research involves the Internet and primary data analysis, but you would also be surprised at how often we learn something about a market or competition in a particular category by studying their local sales efforts. When we are hired to deploy a marketing strategy, we literally leave no stone unturned in becoming experts on markets, competitors, and target audiences—for one client, we invested significant time in the field, researching their stone quarry operations to better understand an operational issue that was restraining a marketing initiative.

The depth of previous experience and new methodology at our firm allows us to sort through any gray areas of target audience behavior to make firm, black-and-white decisions about how best to communicate with them. We often conducted man-in-the-street interviews or mystery shopped our clients' competitors, even requesting proposals from them as we pose as potential customers. Our objective is to see firsthand how they interact with prospects, all in order to confirm, support, or refute the strategic positioning and tactical approach to the market.

We've spent a lot of time talking about how to gather relevant research information to make better decisions about marketing to customers and prospects. In the next chapter about marketing strategy, we'll begin looking at how we analyze the competition, put all the information together, develop the appropriate marketing tactics to harness the power of a brand, and implement a successful marketing plan that propels the message into the minds and hearts of target audiences.

CHAPTER 8—TAKE AWAYS

- It's not just about the right message through the right channel, a message with the right *timing* based on behavioral feedback becomes the greater differentiator (reference graphic on page 133).
- Data segmentation should not be based on demographic segmentation alone. Dynamic segmentation involves sociographics, psychographics, and behavioral interactions combined in real-time with demographic data sets.
- Create your messaging to be as personalized and individually intimate as possible.
- Take the extra step. Create marketing that influences your targets to *feel* something when considering your brand.

CHAPTER 9

Strategy or Tragedy

Mapping your way to the marketplace

Marketing without a strategy is like prospecting without a map—you could lose your ass.

Bob House

© 2010 FabCom. All rights reserved.

Strategy or Tragedy? Mapping Your Way to the Marketplace

Marketing without a strategy is like prospecting without a map, you could lose your ass. It's a strategic tragedy—a stragedy.

No matter the technology or methodology, an intelligent marketing strategy, based on comprehensive research, is the single most important key to successful, high ROI marketing and advertising. That's why I've always been surprised at the amount of marketing that gets done with little or no thought given to first developing a clearly-articulated guiding strategy. In my experience, this is the main reason those with marketing responsibilities have been disappointed in the results achieved by marketing initiatives. Nine out of ten unsuccessful campaigns could have been successful if the strategy had been on target in the first place.

The typical marketing plan begins with a sales increase amount or tactics that are mandated by upper management. The sales increase figure is almost always based on "what we need this year to make our overall numbers," not on an objective look at what could be available or possible, given the current dynamics of the marketplace. Since it's an internal company opinion—"wish" might be a better term—who knows if it's too high or, as is often the case, too low, impossible to achieve, or easy to achieve? It's simply a number picked out of the air because, "that's what we need from marketing and sales."

If a marketing plan is formally written, it usually consists of simple narratives that describe generally the end results of efforts needed to meet the mandated goal: "We need to increase awareness." "We must connect better with our customers." "We need to develop an online presence." Some or all of these could be true in terms of increasing results, but there is usually minimal thinking regarding the specifics of how these goals will be achieved.

So, let's see, unsuccessful campaigns start with an arbitrary goal, list a few hopeful achievements that may help in meeting the goal, don't develop an overall, synergistic plan to accomplish those achievements, and, finally, don't create any meaningful embedded, organic metrics instruments for the achievements that drive progress and profitability. Campaigns that don't meet their objectives do not provide the real-time data required to make week-to-week pivots, to empower the staff in fine-tuning the strategy to achieve the goals, regardless of the conditions or obstacles confronted.

Is it any wonder that business owners and CEOs are not only often disappointed in the results of marketing and advertising, but the whole field seems to be some sort of esoteric and expensive art form rather than a measurable, projectable, ROI-positive function of the business?

On target, insightful strategic thinking, first and foremost, is the only methodology that can reliably and consistently produce lasting, positive results from marketing activity, regardless of industry or target audiences.

Furthermore, a strategic plan enables you continually to know where you are in the process of achieving your goals so that you can make intelligent, on-going fine-tuning adjustments to optimize results. If we are not working from a detailed, comprehensive, coherent plan, we have no "stake in the ground" from which to evaluate progress and make needed changes. When things aren't going right, without a plan, a company may be willing to try anything different in hopes of improvement. With a strategic marketing plan, you can make informed, precise course corrections as needed. Without a plan, you're reduced to guessing what next tactic might be helpful in overcoming challenges and generating positive results. Without a plan, even good ideas may be side-tracked, restrained, or unable to make a positive contribution.

A comprehensive strategic marketing plan is a road map to achieving specific marketing goals over a given period of time. And just like a road map, the more pertinent details that are left out, the less likely you are to arrive at your destination—on time and on budget.

A marketing plan is often confused with an overall corporate strategic business plan. The marketing plan is only one part of the business plan. The objectives and goals of the corporate business plan drive the strategy of the marketing plan. Both plans must be in alignment and synergistic in order to succeed.

A strategic marketing plan brings together the insights of brand positioning, research, and analysis to inform a set of actionable tactics that will drive achievement of its goals based on creating differentiation and competitive advantage in the perceptions of specific target audiences. Keeping in mind, of course, that marketing is only a promise—a promise to all stakeholders. If your interactions do not live up to the perceptions your brand messaging and positioning create, you really don't have the brand you desire and will sooner, rather than later, create negative and deteriorating results.

Every business needs a strategic marketing plan, no matter how large or small the business. For the small business entrepreneur, a plan can harness and focus seat-of-the-pants entrepreneurial drive and energy to more reliably achieve meaningful goals. Fortune 100 corporations could not efficiently, effectively, or profitably deploy their huge marketing resources without a synergistic strategic plan. Without a plan, how will you ever determine which of the 10,000 available marketing tactics are right for your business and your situation? How can you sort the 107 initiatives you must marshal in the next year to drive success out of the 10,000 available tactics? And how will you select tactics to create synergy among them so they work together to optimize progress toward the plan's goals?

One thing I have discovered in my two and a half decades working in the industry is that many companies who profess to have an internal marketing planning process more often than not are unable to implement their plan completely and effectively, let alone fully achieve the goals as stated. Here's my friendly warning to business owners and CEOs about strategic planning, based on consistent experience over the years: Even if you are smart enough and lucky enough to finally have an intelligent plan in hand, you will have a strong tendency to want to cherry pick the tactics that comprise the plan. You will have pet tactics you want to implement for personal or political reasons rather than strategic considerations. Often, decision makers will want to drop certain tactics simply on the basis of cost reduction, without considering the strategic implications in terms of meeting or exceeding overall goals. Remember what Sun Tzu said in his famous book, *The Art of War*: Strategy without tactics is the slowest route to victory. Tactics without strategy is the noise before defeat.

A successful plan—a plan that is likely to achieve its goals—needs a depth of research, analysis, and thought from its creators that generates confidence and commitment on the part of those who will be managing and implementing it. A well-crafted plan is an interlocking, mutually nurturing set of tactics assembled to achieve specific goals. When the dynamics of the tactics are changed, it should be clear that there is potential to reduce the odds of achieving the strategy's goals.

Consistency and commitment are vital to the success of a strategic marketing plan. Successful plans not only have well-researched and thought-out tactics, they also get all stakeholders on the same page for implementation. This ability to prompt everyone moving in the same direction is a powerful aspect of strategic planning. The consensus commitment to a strategy is as much a factor in its ultimate success as is the quality of the individual tactics; neither can be achieved without the other.

Keep in mind that creating a plan and implementing a plan call for very different skill sets. Plan creators are thinkers who can see a future vision and lay out a road map—the strategy— to get there. They can explain the intricacies of the plan in order to bring everyone together and moving in the same direction. Plan implementers need to be enthusiastic, persistent, operationally-savvy self-starters who will not only get behind the plan and buy into its goals, but will also take ownership of their areas of responsibility in the strategy to ensure effective, efficient implementation.

Your SWOT, competition, and your target audience(s) determine the supporting mechanics behind your marketing strategy, just as their perceptions and actions dictate how you can best position your product/service to fill a hole in the market and begin making your way into your audience(s)' mind space. Without competition, there would be no need for strategy.

At our firm, we use a hybrid strategy process that is completed and implemented within sixty days. It begins, as I have said, with extensive research (sometimes referred to as a "deep dive" analysis) that allows us to validate the current state of the market, as well as our client's place within it. We first look externally at competition, target audience(s), the cost to communicate with those audiences on their preferred platform, and the current and near-term (three years) economic environment. Then, we look internally at any restraining forces that might hinder or delay the success of the strategy.

We have already detailed audience research methodologies in earlier chapters, so here I'll give you an overview of some of the ways in which we conduct competitive research to uncover the brand attributes that we can map into granular, relevant, one to one messaging that will be effective.

We first look at the scope of the market and, depending on the current evolutionary stage of the market for a particular product, it may not necessarily be easy to determine its total size with specificity. In those cases, we compile information from several sources and are then able to calculate a confident, reasonable estimate. Once we have a market size we feel is solid, we begin to dissect the various competitors to calculate market share as well as their product specifications, positioning, and claims.

We construct our competitive research on the foundation of the Five Basic Forces of Competition, first modeled by Michael Porter of the Harvard Business School:

- The threat of substitute products
- The threat of the entry of new competitors
- The intensity of competitive rivalry
- The bargaining power of customers
- The bargaining power of suppliers

By researching and analyzing these forces, we can determine not only what a strategy will have to accomplish in order to be successful, but also the relative degree of difficulty in pursuing those accomplishments. Some markets are more difficult than others. For example, many competitors give customers bargaining power they can use against you; if the barrier to entry in your market segment is low, competitors can easily multiply against you. Porter's framework is just that—a beginning point upon which to assemble detailed information from many sources. As I've said before, you can't rely on one or a few data points in building a successful strategy. That's why we also often mystery shop competitors in the market to deepen our understanding before drafting a strategy.

Once we reach definitive conclusions based on our analysis of the target audiences and competitors, we know who we want to talk to and what we need to say. We can then begin to determine the cost associated with an effective marketing communications campaign.

According to the conventional wisdoms of marketing, you have to invest separately for brand development, awareness, and lead generation. This is because one to many messaging requires brand marketing to be generalized in an attempt to attract the most attention without dropping the most number of prospects. The purpose of conventionally coveted awareness marketing is to drive the idea that this particular company or product is good to do business with. And then the lead generation is focused on particular offers that hit a particular target to drive them to action.

Under our new methodology of fully dynamic and integrated one to one marketing, you can accomplish all the missions of the previously mentioned marketing processes without having to invest separately and incrementally to achieve the initial result you are looking for. If integrated dynamic cross-channel, cross-media, one to one marketing campaigns are built properly, then as the customer moves through the cycles, from awareness to consideration to purchase and then finally loyalty, the campaigns offer message progression. Based on the interactivity with the campaign, the marketing platform can tell what messages have been received, what messages must be communicated next, exactly what kind of call to action would be motivating and just the right time to present it. The additional costs of brand mapping and strategic set up are more than offset by the integrated approach to dynamic cross-channel marketing that lowers overall costs per new customer and increases the bottom line return.

Finally, audience research will tell us where to reach the right eyes and/or ears with our message—late night TV, Internet, social media, newspaper or magazine, mobile communication, display, whatever the audience preference, competitors, and targets dictate.

And Don't Forget to Add the Rule of Thumb

Most of us have been lucky enough to have had a mentor at some point in our business careers. Mine was an older gentleman in the publishing business whom I worked for very early in my career. He was a successful businessman and had been so for some time. I figured out that if I watched and listened carefully, I could perhaps pick up knowledge and habits that would help put me on the road to success. One of the powerful things I learned was that a rule of thumb proven over years of experience could be a great time and resource-saving tool. My colleagues and I would spend hours working through a complex calculation to determine the best approach to a problem's solution. When we took it to our seasoned boss to show him how smart we were to figure it out, before we could even begin our self-congratulatory presentation, he would say, "You know, whenever I've faced a challenge like this in my career, I would just apply this rule of thumb." The next words out of his mouth would be a quick summary of the solution we had come up with after hours of mental and mathematical gymnastics. It was not only correct, but often it was a more sufficient solution than we had been able to come up with. In the right hands, with the right experience and perspective, a rule of thumb can be an excellent problem-solving shortcut.

You will hear many rules of thumb about how many times you need to get your message in front of members of the target audience so that it reaches critical mass—the audience sees or hears it enough times that those who are actively considering a purchase in the category at the time of the communication begin to make measurable inquiries. Two rules of thumb that I've found to be realistic over the years are:

1. Over the long term, on average, based on conventional marketing process, you need to touch the prospect with your message twenty-three times to move him or her from "never heard of Acme Brand" to "I need to get some Acme." Not every one of the twenty-three touches is necessarily communication in paid media. Word of mouth about your brand, interaction with an online channel, or a billing inquiry, for example, is a touch that you don't pay for directly. This all adds up if the messaging is mapped to the audience and sequenced properly within the funnel of communications.

2. In the near term, reach and frequency can be good estimating points for what it will take to get your message to enough people so that you can be reasonably assured your campaign of increased inquiries (assuming it's the right message at the right time, of course). Reach is a measure of the portion of your target audience who are exposed to your message in a defined time period. Frequency is a measure of the average number of times each member of the audience hears or sees the message in that period of time.

   Conventional experience says that a reach of 20 percent with a frequency of three or four within a few weeks can, on average, generate measurable results. If 20 percent of your target audience currently considering a purchase in the category hears or sees your message three or four times in three or four weeks, you should see some action—or something is wrong. The target audience may be all female golfers in a metro market or all retirement-aged adults in the western U.S.—the average ratios apply regardless of the size of the audience.

While these rules of thumb are helpful, you must also always look at category-specific economic and other quantifiable data as well as industry-specific projections in researching a strategic marketing plan. Recent years have taught us to make economic projections a higher priority in developing a plan. There will always be ups and downs in the economy, but in those periods in which highs may be particularly high or lows may be at their lowest, a successful plan will help predict and prepare for those possibilities and will certainly allow for more intelligent, less costly, faster reactions when challenges arise.

Once we have compiled and analyzed the data from as many different sources and perspectives as possible, we can then form preliminary ideas about the nature of the market and the strategy required to advance a client's interests in that environment. We then sit down with key stakeholders within the organization to gather their perceptions, insights, and reactions to key target audiences, competition, past activity, and other internal issues that may bear on the structure of the strategy or specific tactics. This is a wide-ranging, very targeted and prepared discussion that typically lasts six or more hours as we move back and forth from big picture to detail view in order to gain a clear and actionable view of the company, all its leaders' beliefs, and the company's place in the market.

Here is another rule of thumb that has proven to be true for company after company, regardless of size or industry: In a well run company, 80 percent of everything a company's leaders believe to be true about their company, its products, services, and people is absolutely true—20 percent is 180° opposite.

It is within this 20 percent of misperception that the golden nuggets of truth and great corporate gains are found with outside-in thinking. With a poorly run company, one that is losing money or market share consistently, the figure of what they believe is solid and true is 50 percent. Fifty percent of their beliefs and resulting actions are accurate, and 50 percent of their beliefs are inaccurate and more than 90 percent off on the reality of the market and their company's place within the minds of the target audience.

Now that we have all the quantitative and qualitative data, the analysis becomes the critical starting point for strategic thinking. It is imperative that a good marketer separate events, trends, challenges, opportunities, and projections into their component parts so that we can determine the precise significance of each of the components. Then we re-assemble them in a way calculated to maximize the competitive advantage.

At this point, we begin to develop the goals and objectives for the strategy in conjunction with the client's team. Goals must be realistic, specific, measurable, and relevant. Objectives in the strategy are similar except they are designed as intermediate accomplishments to the goals. Along with an analysis of the market and target audiences, these strategic elements comprise the spine of the strategy. We then begin to develop messaging and creative to build an implementable, accountable, successful overall strategy.

Innovative strategy, complemented by experience and science, is used to optimize communication and delivery of messaging to very specific target audiences. Our team's ability to consistently produce improved marketing results for our clients is grounded in a strategic culture, innovation and creativity. The methodology is enhanced with a scientific approach to data and a unique depth of experience.

Over the years, we have developed and refined an optimization equation to express our strategic thinking and methodology to optimize the content and individual messaging, imagery, and call to action for dynamic one to one marketing.

The specific Strategic Methodology for optimized content grows out of the larger Strategic Workflow we utilize to uncover and scrutinize any information that may be useful in developing a client's comprehensive marketing plan.

The Science of Brand Mapping

How exactly do we execute the proliferation of additional research, image, message, and call to action variable nature of dialogic micro marketing in real-time with real-world objectives and real outcomes? By laying it all out in a reproduce-able formula that configures a mapping for every honestly appearing natural brand element that also connects to your target audiences' behaviors, physiographic and demographics attributes, combined with place in the buying cycle. This not-so-simple equation distills all the moving parts into a single, unified system for brand mapping, which, when followed correctly and without compromise, will deliver the exponential returns of Neuromarketology™.

All the pieces of the puzzle are accounted for, from planning, organizational goals and research, to target profiling, target messaging, and real-time accountability. Note how deep into the process we go before we even start creative development? This is what it means to be strategic in the new marketing paradigm in which we find ourselves.

Strategic is one of the most overused terms in advertising. It generally means some thought on some level is given to the outcomes desired before the creatives cut loose and do their thing. In the new world of Neuromarketology™, being strategic means shaping every piece of creative and messaging to each segment, targeted and defined to the nth degree (the N of course standing for Neuromarketology™). The result is optimized messaging, another overused piece of ad lingo, which in our world means real, measurable hyper-relevance. Going all the way back to the first chapter, this is the equation that delivers that lucrative one in ten response, instead of the rather dismal two out of a hundred.

The accompanying workflow strategy shows precisely how we can execute this on behalf of our clients in just sixty days. It's a thing of beauty, not just to our team who developed it, but to all marketers seeking to step up to this new, more relative and productive paradigm.

In a successful strategic planning process:

- Goals are specific, measurable, achievable, relevant, and **tangible business objectives**.
- Strategies are the **ideas and approaches** that are developed to achieve the goals.
- Tactics are the **specific actions, details,** and **activities** that must occur in order for the strategy to succeed.

Strategic Methodology

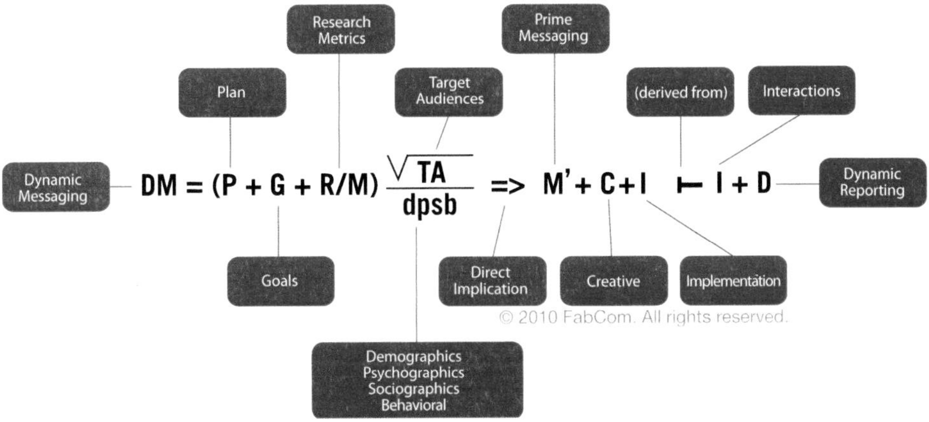

Strategic Workflow

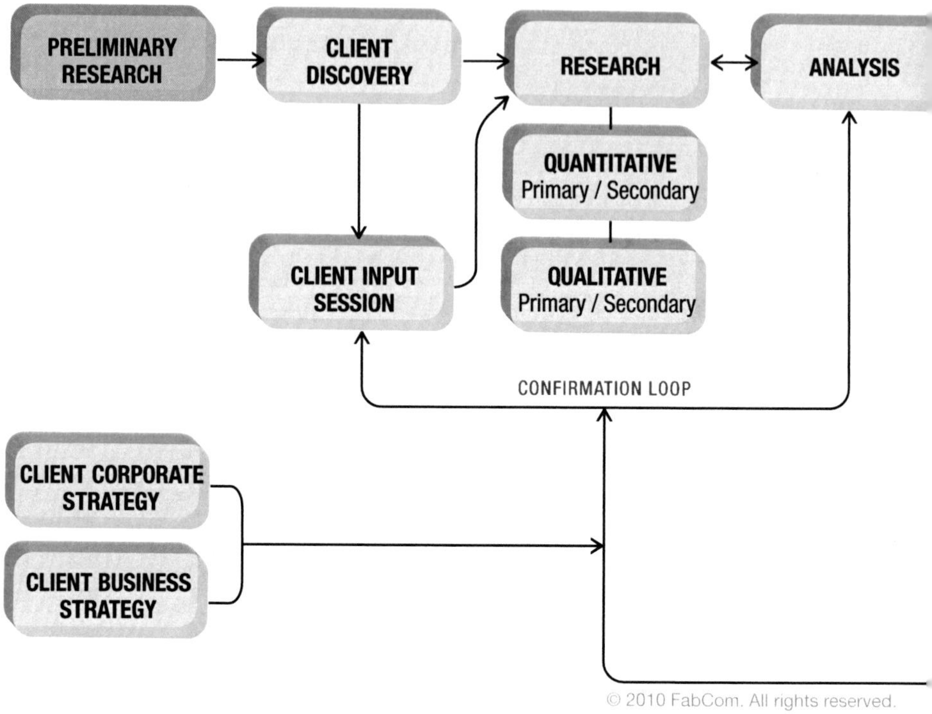

Strategic workflow that drives the marketing strategy and campaign development.

Note that the strategic workflow is a complete loop that uses metrics and accountability to ensure on-going process improvement and fine-tuning of tactics.

You can also see that a successful marketing plan addresses corporate and business strategies to ensure that we consider all the business

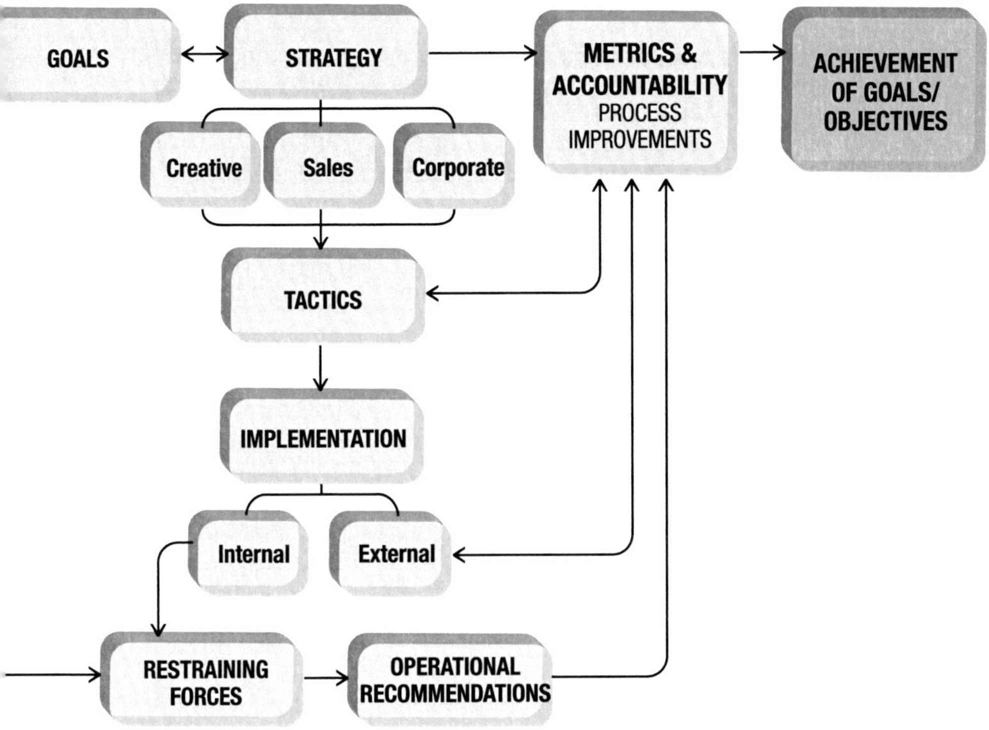

and operational implications of the strategy and tactics developed. We must be certain that the strategic marketing plan converges with and augments the company operations and administrative functions or it will never be fully or properly implemented. In this regard, we look for restraining forces within the client company that may hinder the implementation of the strategy. When we identify restraining forces, we make operational recommendations to resolve the restraining challenges. Many times these restraining forces and countering recommendations lie outside the scope of what would normally be considered marketing functions. It is critical to have a depth of *business management* experience in addition to specific marketing expertise in order to uncover inevitable operational and/or administrative business issues that may have the potential to derail the strategy. It is also critical to address them up front in the creation of the strategy, well before the implementation.

But, How Much do I Invest?

The question that I am most often asked regarding strategic marketing is also the most basic question about the topic: how much should I spend on marketing? Over the years, any number of general estimates on the correct amount to invest in marketing have been developed. You will hear that in your type of business you should spend 5 percent of gross revenues or 10 percent of your net or some such general percentage. While I have found these general rules to be useful in helping a client estimate their marketing budget, like all general rules they are just, well, general. I prefer to look at the specifics of a client's situation and make a budget calculation that can tie back to return on investment, so that we have a foundation upon which we can build metrics for monitoring the progress of strategic implementation.

Let me describe the calculation I go through in marketing budgeting and then I'll show you an example of the calculation in action. Again, keep in mind this is a useful rule of thumb, not a scientific formula that can be applied to all situations. You need to start with two pieces of data: "Where are you now?" (What is current gross margin on revenue or sales?), and "Where do you want to be one year from now?" (What would you like the gross margin to be as a result of growing sales?). We usually ask clients "Where would you like to be in one year?" and "Where do you think you might be in one year if you do nothing different from you are now?" Consistently, clients project that, even though their business is not currently performing the way they would like, the business will grow 10 percent or more in the next year. I guess the poet was right when he said, ". . . hope springs eternal." When we question clients about how could their business grow 10 percent in a year if they continue to do exactly what they are doing now, they always have some kind of hopeful justification for why it will get better. We have to tell them that their results are extremely unlikely to change if they don't change anything in their business. Psychiatrists have a term for people who do the same things over and over expecting to get different results each time—crazy. Occasionally, however, there is some real-world reason why your company might grow if you do nothing new (change in government regulations, a competitor going out of business, etc.). In that case, the growth should be factored into your scenario.

Back to our calculation, once you know where you are and where you want to be, you can calculate the difference between the two, or the amount your business will need to grow in the next year to achieve your estimated goal. That figure is your goal for incremental gross margin growth. We know from experience that if a client does a good job of implementing the plan we create, the tactics executed should be able to generate a 3:1 or 4:1 return on investment. That tells me that a client will need to invest between 25 percent and 30 percent of their goal for incremental revenue growth to achieve it. Here's an example of the calculation:

A.	Where you are now (relative to gross margin)?	$100
B.	Where would you like to be in twelve months?	$150
C.	Goal for incremental growth	$50
D.	Assume a 4:1 return on marketing	$50/4
E.	Marketing budget to achieve gross margin goal	$12.5

In other words, if you want to grow your gross margin on sales by $50,000 over the next year, you would need to invest $12,500 in marketing budget. Or, on a larger stage, if you want to grow gross margin on sales by $50 million over the next year, you should plan on a sales and marketing budget of $12.5 million—the calculation remains the same.

You may feel that investing 25 percent of the margin growth you would like to achieve sounds expensive, but when you look at it as a 4:1 return on your investment, you can hardly complain. Where else can you get a 400 percent return on your money today? The example is assuming a 50 percent gross margin on product sales.

I'm going to close this chapter on strategic marketing with a case study that demonstrates the impact of applying strategic thinking to marketing.

A university focused on leading edge technology came to us because their enrollment numbers had plateaued and nothing they did could get them moving upward. We took a hard look at their entire marketing communications system and found two fatal flaws that were holding them back. First flaw: They were prospecting only in their own backyard, a metropolitan market that didn't have an especially high propensity for high school students to go on to a private local college. Even more detrimental to enrollment, they were only communicating with high school seniors or older.

Our strategy recommended two tactics to align the client's marketing behavior with the behavior of the market. We re-targeted marketing communications to prospects in markets or states where more high school students go on to college rather than exclusively in the university's hometown market. In addition to greatly expanding the pool of potential students, this also put our client's private university tuition in a more positive light, as out of state tuition, which actually compared favorably with our client's tuition. We simply helped level the field with the targeting.

Most importantly, we helped design and implement a new marketing communications system/enrollment funnel that began talking to high school students in their sophomore year—when they first begin to think seriously about going to college, not in their senior year when the students most serious about college have already made their college choice.

The result? Inquiries immediately shot up, followed by an increase in applications and (can you see where this is going?) enrollment for the very next semester increased 20 percent. Seven years—and three strategic marketing plans—later, the university has increased their enrollment, retention, and substantially increased the tuition they are able to charge. Needless to say, they are still happy clients of our firm.

I'll wrap up this chapter with one of my favorite quotes about strategy, from Winston Churchill: "However beautiful the strategy, you should occasionally look at the results."

As we discussed at the beginning of this chapter, no matter the technology or methodology, an intelligent marketing strategy, based on comprehensive research, is the single most important key to successful, high ROI marketing and advertising. No amount of advanced technology or sophisticated methodologies can optimize your marketing results if it is not driven by innovative, strategic thinking and judged by accurate, timely metrics.

CHAPTER 9—TAKE AWAYS

- Start first with a written comprehensive marketing strategy with each element, strategy, and tactic built to be measurable.
- Treat your finished plan just like a roadmap. Check it often—daily and weekly at the minimum.
- Remember what Sun Tzu teaches in his book: Strategy without tactics is the slowest route to victory. Tactics with strategy is the noise before defeat.

- Deploying a strategic marketing plan requires a myriad of different skill sets. Align your resources before deployment.
- On target strategy is half the battle; experienced implementation of a strategy is the other half. Both must be maintained for success.
- Remember the 80/20 rule of strategic planning: In a well-run company, 80 percent of everything a company's leaders believe to be true about their company, its products, services, and people is absolutely true—20 percent is 180 degrees opposite. Your job as a marketing leader is to find the 20 percent and fix it!
- Great strategy takes quantitative, qualitative, innovative, linear, lateral, and creative thinking. Then those thoughts must be woven into the fabric of the corporate S.W.O.T. to engineer a proper implementation plan.
- There are ten critical steps of thought progression that are necessary before the messaging and creative can even be considered when developing messaging for a relevant dynamic one to one communication. (See chart on page 151.)

CHAPTER 10

Micro Conversations

Dialogic marketing made automated

So far, we've looked at a number of elements that are key to successful marketing in today's rapidly-changing, dynamic, multi-media, multi-platform, fragmented audience world: brand and positioning, Neuromarketology™, comprehensive market research, objective, strategic thinking, technology, and a leading edge methodology to harness the strategy and technology. These are the pillars upon which smart modern marketers can build effective, accountable marketing campaigns to meet today's new and rapidly evolving challenges to deliver sales results, brand growth, and return on investment. Understanding and successfully applying these concepts to your organization, guided by an intelligent marketing strategy, can bring you the return on investment from your marketing investments that the industry leaders achieve.

What other forces are already driving the *future* of marketing? What new opportunities are becoming available right now and in the future? In a sentence, more channels, more fragmentation, and more opportunity for the smart marketer who knows how to parse and free your actionable data. This can be accomplished by harnessing the new technology and incorporating the tried and true laws of marketing with innovative strategies.

Not surprisingly, regardless of all the developments, the number one rule of thumb for marketing will continue to be: Anticipate and react to what the customer wants. Be more relevant to your targets than your competition is.

Going forward, as we've seen, there will continue to be more and more choices for engaging the customer with marketing relevancy. While the ever-exploding number of marketing channels offers new opportunities, these multiplying media channels require far more personalized communications (also known as dynamic or one to one marketing) to help the consumer sort through the deluge of marketing messaging. This continued progression of marketing channels will also make delivering the right message to the right person at the right time in the right place even more critical and challenging—unless you have the methodology and technology to *automate* the process of dynamic one to one marketing versus conventional one to many marketing.

The future opportunities lie in combining strategic thinking and advancing technology. This allows those firms that have the resources to deploy that technology to implement true end-to-end, dynamic marketing systems that can reliably deliver on the promise of the right message to the right person at the right time in the right place. Advancing technology and the ability to optimize and automate marketing communications processes is the topic of this chapter. First, we need to understand the global trends that will make state-of-the-art marketing technology the key issue for marketing success and continued growth in the future.

"The evolution from mass to micromarketing is a fundamental change."

- Business Week

"The advertising industry is going through one of the most disorienting periods in its history." - Economist.com

© Business Week magazine, The McGraw-Hill Companies, Inc.

"The driver for demand going forward is all about products that are 'right for me.'" - Interbrand

Today's customers—both business and consumer—are demanding that marketers and manufacturers meet their personal needs and specifications. Several decades of consumer-tailored advertising and a long line of significant cultural shifts have led to markets in which everyone wants to be treated as an individual, with solutions (products or services) personalized for their specific situation. Micromarketing is the term used to describe customizing products and marketing campaigns specifically for individuals in the target audience. Segmentation is the basic methodology we use to do it systematically. As we have seen in previous chapters, micromarketing requires a higher level of understanding and knowledge about customers and prospects.

The rise of micromarketing has also come about as a response to the double-edged sword of the decreased effectiveness and rising cost of traditional, mostly TV and print-based mass marketing, as shown in the chart below:

AC Nielsen Corp., Universal McCann, independent research

*2012 Projection By FabCom.

The trend toward a highly individualized and personalized marketplace was identified as *The Long Tail* in Chris Anderson's 2006 book of the same name. A group of researchers (Erik Brynjolfsson, Yu Hu, and Michael D. Smith) first used a "Long Tail" graph (see chart on next page) to describe the relationship between Amazon.com sales and Amazon sales ranking. They discovered the largest proportion of Amazon.com's book sales come from obscure books that are not available in brick-and-mortar bookstores. This turns the old 80/20 rule of thumb on its head when the total sales profit of the 80 percent of less popular or more obscure items exceeds the total sales profit of the 20 percent top-selling products. Where we used to concentrate marketing resources on that 20 percent of best-selling items because it represented greater profit potential, the advent of the Internet and its ability to inexpensively offer vast choice to the buying public means that The Long Tail—the 80 percent of slower-selling items—can now be a potentially larger source of profit for sellers.

As an example, Amazon offers books that are on the *New York Times* list of today's best sellers, as well as copies of books that may have been out of print for forty years or more and very specialized new technical books (like this one) with small audiences. Previously, the 80/20 rule would have told Amazon to focus their efforts and resources on selling more of the best sellers. Today, with millions of book lovers going online all over the world to find out-of-print and obscure titles, assisted by search engines and aggregator websites, total profit from the sale of these books is actually higher than the profit from the sale of typically deeply discounted, warehoused, and shelved brick-and-mortar-found best sellers. That's why some refer to The Long Tail phenomenon as "selling more of less." Indeed, one Amazon executive, quoted on Wired.com, described the effect as, "We sold more books today that didn't sell at all yesterday than we sold today of all the books that did sell yesterday." The graph below illustrates this relationship between popularity and inventory, such as Amazon's book inventory or Netflix's movie inventory.

Long Tail Graph

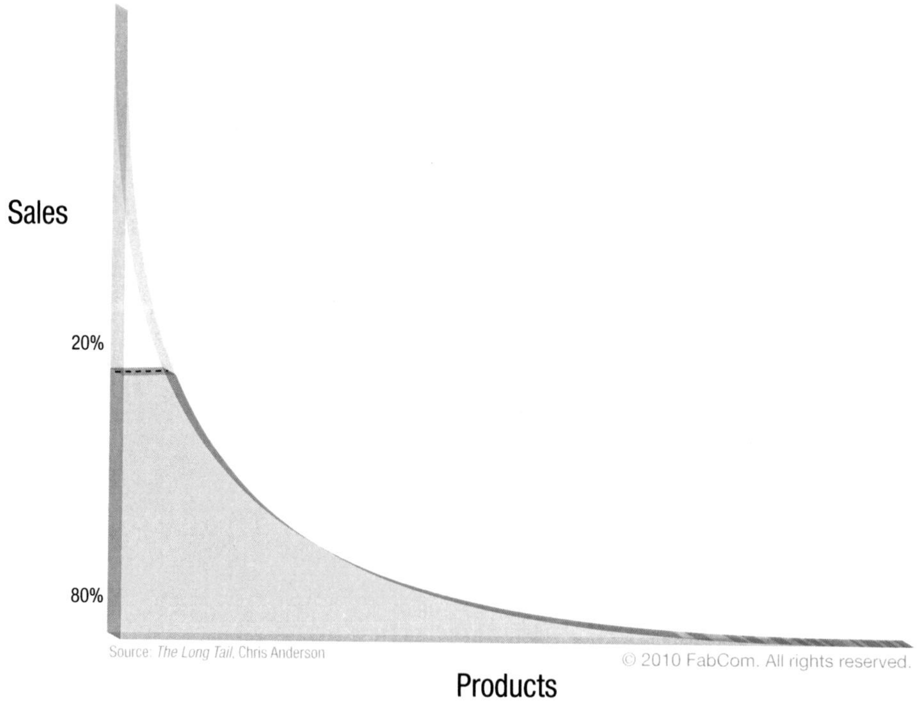

NOTE TO READER: In order to truly leverage the power of Neuromarketology™ as a strategy, please read Chris Anderson's *The Long Tail.*

The Long Tail online business model has potential for many marketers. The distribution and sales channel opportunities created by the connectivity of the Internet and increased bandwidth capacity often enable businesses to tap into that marketing model successfully. The Long Tail concept can be used to understand that the primary value of the Internet to consumers and businesses comes from releasing new sources of value and revenue by providing access to lower demand products.

The key factor that determines whether a particular sales distribution has a Long Tail is the cost of inventory storage and distribution. If inventory storage and distribution costs are insignificant, it becomes economically viable to sell relatively unpopular products. If storage and distribution costs are high, only the most popular products can be sold. An *MIT Sloan Management Review* article, titled, "From Niches to Riches: Anatomy of *The Long Tail*," examines *The Long Tail* from the demand side and the supply side and identifies key drivers. For the supply side, the authors point out how e-tailers' expanded, centralized warehousing allows for more product offerings and makes it possible for them to profitably cater to more diverse tastes. For the demand side, tools such as search engines, aggregator sites, and sampling tools allow customers to easily find and buy products outside their geographic area.

And all of these big, recent trends in customer/prospect behavior, expectations, and communication platforms that drive the trend toward micromarketing lead us back to two enduring truths we discussed earlier in the book:

- The more personally and intimately marketing communications can be customized for each recipient, the more effective and persuasive they will be. Accomplishing this requires specific methodology to enable precise, narrow segmentation of target audiences and the ability to deliver individualized communications efficiently.

- Even as much as the environment has changed in the last several years, successful marketing still comes down to a core ability to communicate and connect with prospects and customers by reaching:

    A. The Right Audience with

    B. The Right Delivery Channel with

    C. The Right Message with

    D. The Right Timing.

All of which requires a keen mastery of technological horsepower and best practice marketing experience. It also requires complex, multi-variable database analysis accomplished dynamically—what the data gurus refer to as "data deep diving." Huge amounts of data need sophisticated software, powered by extraordinary computing capability and experts experienced in mathematics, programming, and IT, as well as comprehensive strategic thinking. This technology was not affordably available to marketers even just a couple of years ago. Today, it is still demanding in terms of the budget for those that try to re-invent the wheel and the cross-disciplined expertise that is required to deploy it.

My experience, right up to the week I am writing this chapter, is that many professionals in marketing are not fully aware of these latest developments in marketing-related technology and efficiency. Many who say they *are* familiar with the state-of-the-art in this area, don't fully *get* it, thinking that this technology breakthrough is simply a new face and a few hot buzzwords pasted on long-existing computing capabilities. A batch email to a subgroup of your mailing list is *not* what we're talking about and will not get the job done. Therefore, I want to start this discussion of leading-edge marketing technology by laying the foundation for a fuller understanding of what is available to marketers today.

Perhaps the most common name given to the new marketing technology tools available today is "marketing automation," which some refer to as "dialogue marketing." Even that term is not truly expressive of the type of dynamic, end-to-end, cross-media, cross-platform, one to one, micromarketing integrated system that delivers the phenomenal promise of true automated marketing. However, looking back at that fourteen-word, multi-comma, multi-hyphen description in the previous sentence, maybe we should just call it "dynamic marketing automation," for the sake of brevity.

When we say end-to-end system, we are describing a single, efficient workflow delivering a uniquely segmented dialogue with target audiences from planning, to creative execution, through implementation, and finally, the measurement of results in *real-time*. This system encompasses both marketing management (budgeting, planning, creative/production development, and digital asset creation and management, tracking and reporting results in real-time, and so forth) and customer/prospect engagement across a wide range of marketing channels (traditional media as well as website, email, PURLs, mobile, social, and many more—anything that displays/transmits digital information). It's a single integrated system leveraging your siloed data, customers' behaviors and interactions while improving efficiency and control of:

- **Marketing personalization,** customization, and timing, including communications triggered by a customer/prospect's own activity or other defined environmental events (dynamic segmentation).
- **Measurement**—reactive, real-time dynamic dashboards aggregating the results and interactions of all of your siloed marketing programs and disconnected suppliers/initiatives.
- **Accountability**—transparency created by tracking each and every leg of a campaign's costs and output in real-time.
- **Optimized targeting**—allows for automated, self-selected segmentation capability not previously possible with conventional one to many advertising messages. Due to the method of assembling intelligence into the advertising/prospect interactions (now being referred to as transactional, trigger, or dialogue marketing) and the ability to instantly share that information with pre-built, customized-to-individual-target responses, the targeting (sub-group selections for down-line processing) becomes refined by the customer's own responses to the initial touch.
- **Communication**—because of the ability to granularly target segment and the ability to instantaneously draw from a pre-defined set of templates, triggered by a database of if/then protocols, the relevancy of the marketing can be enthralling to the recipients of the message. For instance, in the one to many method of marketing, one might craft a message "for better health . . . try this" or perhaps

segment a blind mailing to target those that are interested in a particular type of better health, all the while eliminating those targets who are not interested precisely in the selected item or any of the selected messaging. With the ability to replace copy, imagery, and calls to action dynamically within each message based on the prospects' hierarchy of needs in real-time, online or offline, the communication becomes a dialogue of relevancy with that particular target versus a one to many message that requires a good amount of blind luck to be relevant to all but the average of that 2 percent return. For example, rather than sending a one to many message with three different offers to try to appeal to the broadest range of recipients on your list, you can send each individual on the list a one to one message containing the one offer that is most appealing to each individual, based on their prior activity or stage in the marketing cycle. This individualized, personal relevancy is the key to increased response and purchase.

- **Delivery**—of the message is dynamically chosen by the behavior of the prospect or customer. If the target reacted first to an online message by responding online, then the corresponding marketing would be continued online unless the target chooses a mix of communications through multiple touch points. If they do, then we serve it up to them in that way. Conversely, if the message that elicited their response reached them via text or smart phone messaging, then you can respond back to them by the same channel (and this would apply to print and offline responses as well).

Remember, it is not so much about merely publishing *to* your customer; it is more about creating a dialogue *with* your customer.

With marketing's new found capability, we no longer must send a series of offers to the customer and hope that one motivates them to buy. We can now efficiently, and with consistency, send a specific offer to each customer that we are confident will be personally relevant to them, based on their previous interactions with your company and others and/or the real-time interactions with your promotions.

Creating hyper-relevance in each and every prospect/customer interaction answers the key question for them—"Is this product or service right for me?" Hyper-relevance results in more respondents, and that translates to:

- More efficient marketing—lower costs
- More effective marketing—improved results
- More customers
- More repeat-purchase customers
- More revenue
- More profit
- More marketing budget
- Improved control and planning

At the risk of repeating myself, this is truly a breakthrough in our capability as marketers to dynamically create, dynamically distribute, control, and measure in real-time the return of marketing and advertising campaigns. It's better, more effective marketing, created with less reliance on human follow-through and more resonance with your targets, and tracked in the same finite, precise manner you expect in every other part of your organization.

How much do I believe that this is the vision of the future when it comes to marketing success, return on investment, and ultimately, survival? Recently, I invested 50 percent of our company's worth in this technology. We have had two banner years in growth back to back, the best of our twenty years in business. Our clients' campaigns results speak for themselves, and it is hard to keep superior returns a secret.

Throughout my career, I have successfully pursued a strategy of differentiating our company and creating competitive advantage by being the first to exploit technology innovations and then adding market share because we became known as the most experienced (best) in the emerging field. Time after time, we have created superior returns by investing to offer a higher quality and more efficient methodology, by staying on the leading edge of technology, ahead of the pack. By the time the pack catches up, we are on to the next extension of that technology. By investing to become a leader in marketing automation technology and, specifically, the strategic and content development specialists and implementation experts for dynamic marketing cross-channel, we believe we have positioned our firm for years to come. A handful of other innovative agencies in the U.S. and internationally can also deploy this technology to similar effect.

But be cautious of those who claim to have this capability but do not; there are many of them out in the marketplace. The objective is to map your brand attributes onto each of your potential segments and then provide the content and platform to present those if/then variables to achieve a deeper resonance with the prospect than your competitors do. Automated email is *not* what we are discussing here. Buying a database software solution to use as a CRM does not unlock those returns without the thinking and content development and brand mapping. We are discussing **dynamic database marketing across all channels, with a centralized, aggregated, real-time intelligence that takes all previous and real-time interactions into account and disseminates a personally-relevant message to each recipient in real-time, with automation, across all the communication channels without bearing the traditional costs associated with custom creation of each and every interaction with the prospect.**

With this thinking and process in place, we can ensure our stakeholders better and more efficient marketing communications and campaign management across all the channels and platforms with which we're confronted today.

This new technology and the wisdom resulting from decades of experience deploying campaigns under the old technology platforms, plus the last few years of testing, investing, and configuring have given some businesses the capability to synchronize data in real-time between sales, marketing, customer service, and, as necessary, other departments throughout the organization to create more audience-relevant content—communications, presentations, sales tools, promotional materials, and advertising. This new methodology, with its ability to provide real-time aggregated reporting across every piece in your marketing funnel, provides marketing decision makers with the ability to make better decisions, creating more flexibility and faster response to changes in market conditions. We can further increase the measurable effectiveness and efficiency of campaigns throughout the entire sales and customer lifecycle.

Let's take a look at the benefit of that synchronicity—how advancing technology can help neutralize the challenges of today's rapidly evolving markets—with three diagrams showing the progression of the Customer Lifecycle:

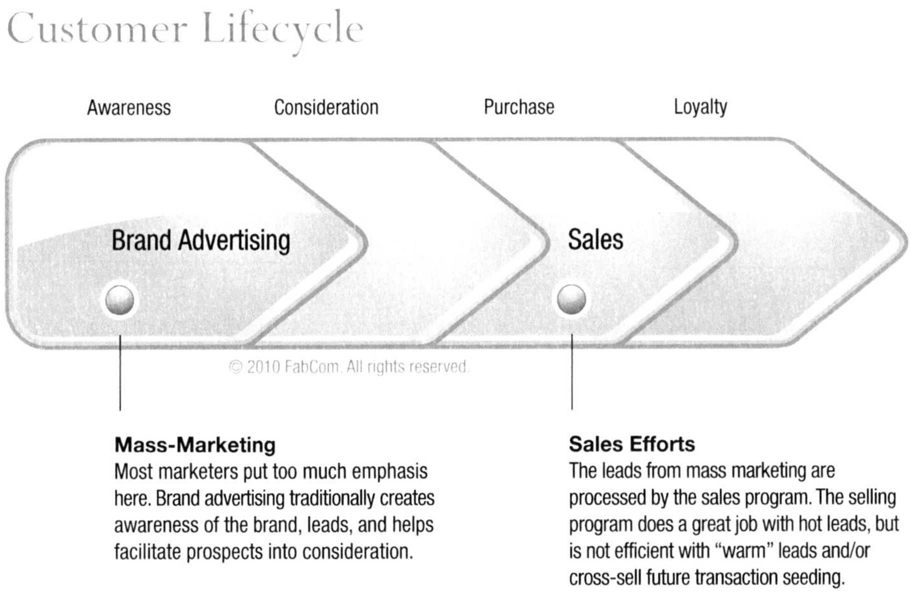
Customer Lifecycle
Awareness
Consideration
Purchase
Loyalty
Brand Advertising
Sales
© 2010 FabCom. All rights reserved.
Mass-Marketing
Most marketers put too much emphasis here. Brand advertising traditionally creates awareness of the brand, leads, and helps facilitate prospects into consideration.
Sales Efforts
The leads from mass marketing are processed by the sales program. The selling program does a great job with hot leads, but is not efficient with "warm" leads and/or cross-sell future transaction seeding.

Consideration Phase

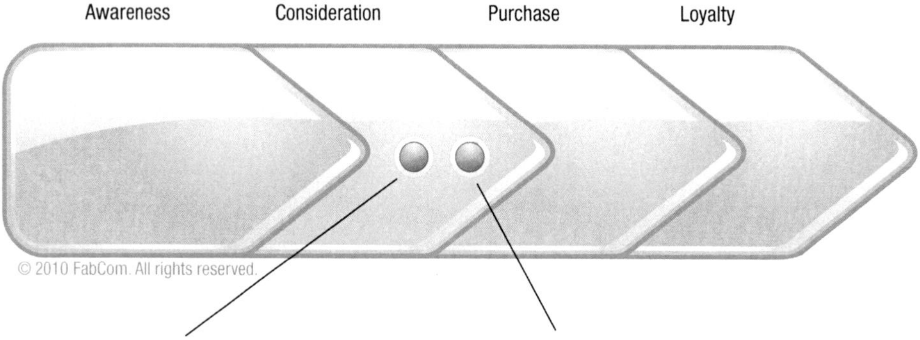

"Google Generation"
Customers are taking control of the consideration phase with self discovery research. New opportunities—yes, but the shift leaves risk that a company's **best story is never heard** and never delivered.

The Self-Servicing of America
Sales has the primary burden of "closing" people in the consideration phase. Yet, complexity of product offerings, and declining sales acumen, are leaving **customers on their own to say "This is for me."**

Micromarketing

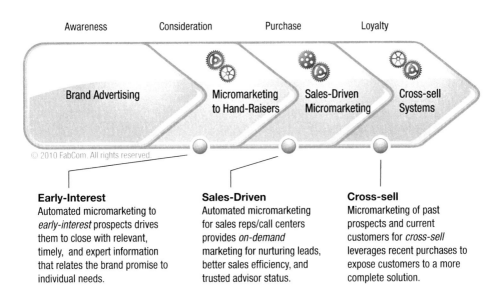

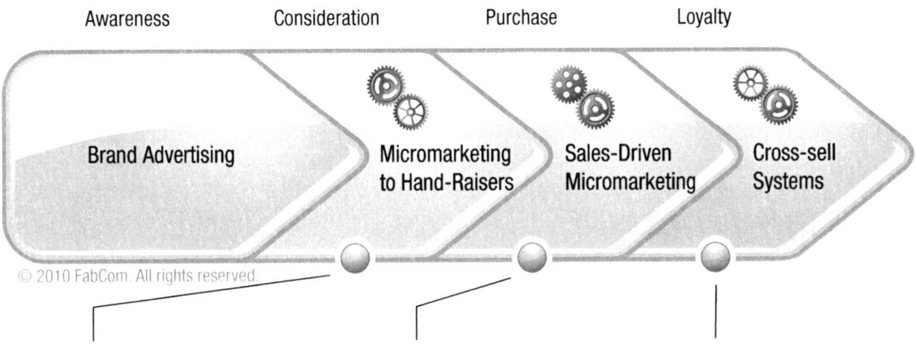

Early-Interest
Automated micromarketing to *early-interest* prospects drives them to close with relevant, timely, and expert information that relates the brand promise to individual needs.

Sales-Driven
Automated micromarketing for sales reps/call centers provides *on-demand* marketing for nurturing leads, better sales efficiency, and trusted advisor status.

Cross-sell
Micromarketing of past prospects and current customers for *cross-sell* leverages recent purchases to expose customers to a more complete solution.

Because we now have both the technology and the what-to-look-for expertise required to generate discrete, actionable tactics and messaging from deep, complex data analyses, we can more accurately and productively segment audiences to execute highly-targeted campaigns. Our firm also deploys a hybrid system we call "ROI Console," which all our clients are provided at no cost the day they hire our agency. This system helps us efficiently map their brand attributes through our strategic methodology described earlier in this book, and then combine that with the positioning and messaging required to outflank each competitor in each prospect pool. Because the metrics are built into our system from the beginning, in creative development and within the base code of each marketing element, we can precisely track, analyze, and manage leads and other results to accurately measure return on investment from individual vehicles and tactics, as well as overall campaigns—online, offline, in the store, contact center, or with the sales staff in real-time.

Leveraging Workflow

Here's an overview of the fundamental components of the end-to-end marketing automation system. At the core of the system are the client's enterprise computer system(s) and the marketing partners' activity, planning, executing, managing, and measuring the campaign tactics through database, CRM, and fulfillment processes.

Leveraging Workflow

One to one marketing structure

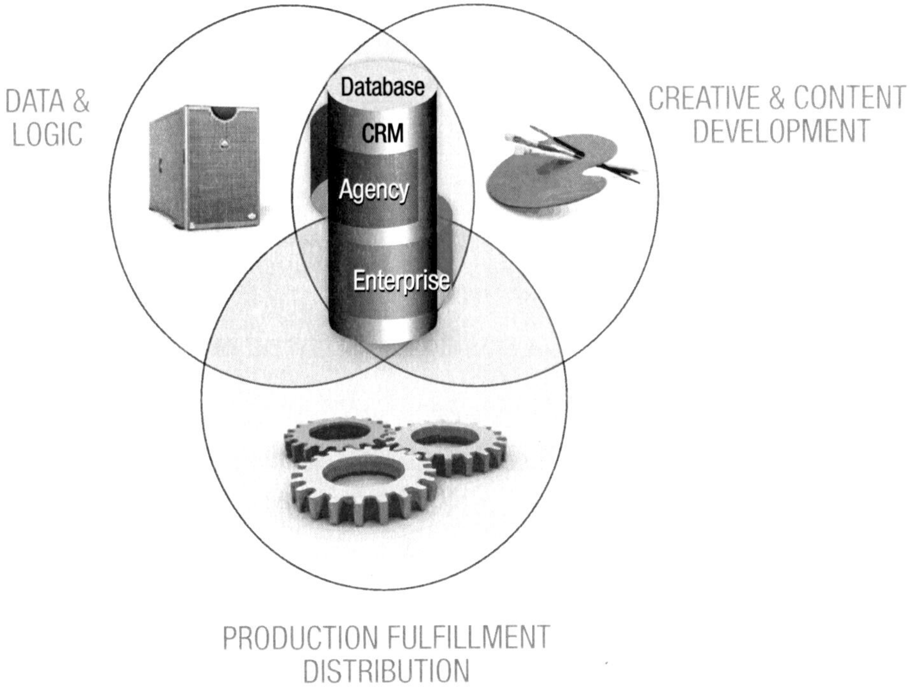

DNA to One to One Micromarketing

There are five main elements that the system auto-integrates in creating each dynamic media campaign:

- **Strategy:** plan and purpose
- **Logic + Business/Transaction Rules:** timing
- **Data:** ability to purpose either Complex or Flat Databases in real-time with no interaction with other personnel or processes with conflicting priorities.
- **Content Development:** dynamically assembled electronically based on the prospects' interactions.
- **Distribution:** ability to disseminate unilaterally, in real-time, marketing assets across all channels that accept a digital file or the result of a digital file.

End-to-End Marketing Workflow

The next diagram illustrates the relationship of the various functions in the end-to-end system we have developed, called ROI Console. As always, we begin with research and strategy—goals, tactics, and metrics. Content (graphics, copy, video, audio, web elements) is created one time and warehoused digitally for dynamic re-purposing online and offline, across campaigns distributed on any platform or media with real-time dynamic reporting. Appropriate outside supplier resources are utilized as necessary and then customized content is efficiently delivered—according to rule-defined timing—to individuals in target audiences across every medium and platform. These activities proceed automatically, in real-time, to generate, motivate, and manage leads, and drive sales. In the closed-loop system, results from tactical execution feed into campaign and customer relationship management processes to continually refine the quality of data available for decisions.

End-to-End Marketing Solution

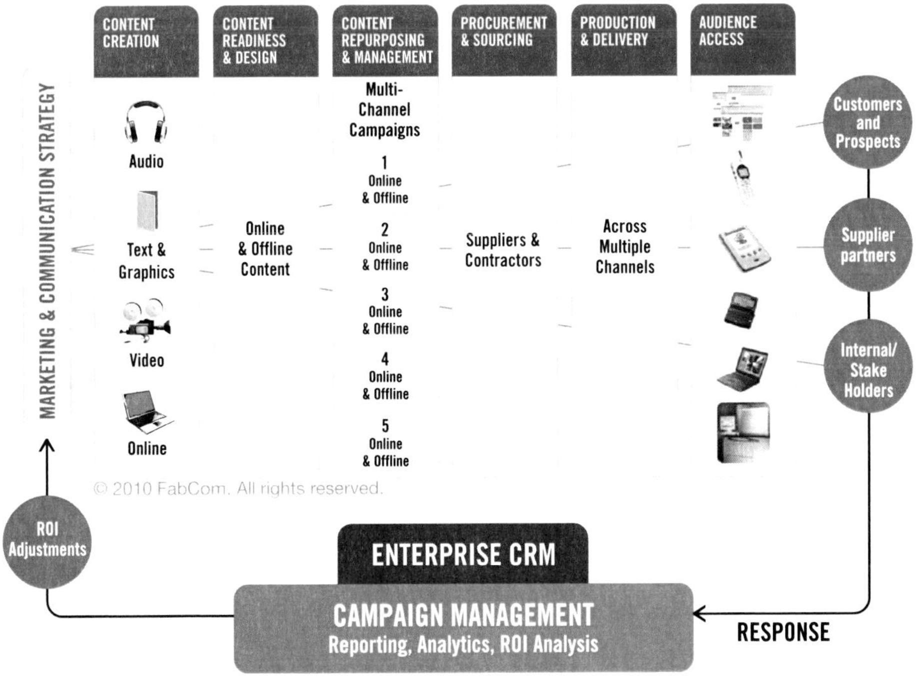

Share Data Don't Integrate

The trick in building a fully dynamic workflow is the way in which we share data and imagery among the needs of the different communication channels. A functioning end-to-end workflow must be designed and configured to work with any existing system by means of web services (the secure communication protocols used to communicate between servers or computers) and "APIs" (specific code that *links* together information from applications or databases). It is important to note up front that nothing in your existing system needs to be replaced. This new approach is a foundational pillar of Neuromarketology™ implementation. This is how we free your data in real-time and link together the siloed data from your target audience's individual interactions with your brand. These can include disparate suppliers, disconnected marketing initiatives (events, trade shows, loyalty programs, etc.), online interactivity, call centers, in-store transactions, sales force activities, distribution and fulfillment centers, basically anything online or offline—utilizing *any* system.

The methodology of *sharing* the output from system to system is the game changer that makes the newer approach to integration work with legacy, state-of-the-art enterprise, or small business systems. I often hear how clients have taken on data integration projects in the past and had miserable outcomes. This is part of the reason we have worked so hard the last few years to break through the conventional thinking to arrive at an alternate methodology to get to our clients' data without having to go through the guardians of data retrieval or the security, operational, and lead time liability of conventional IT integration projects.

Business has always looked at data as a way to measure what *has been done* in the past, not as a way to fine-tune activities in real-time. Even in marketing we have always used trend analysis of past activity to predict future activity. Once data is made available in real-time to us, it becomes another compounding game changer. You strategize differently, you create differently, you communicate differently, and you achieve different results. We must check at the door all we believe to be possible in the area of data repurposing. A new route is possible for an old task that opens up possibilities and efficiencies that were never feasible in the old way of looking at things. (Remember the changing of CDs stored in the trunk of your car, before MP3 players.)

One of my favorite movies of all time is *Dead Poets Society* with Robin Williams. In the movie, Robin Williams plays a professor at a small prep school for privileged students. In one of the most memorable scenes in the movie, Williams sets up a simple experiment for the students, asking them to look at an object on a desk and clearly articulate what they see. Emphatically the students all agree on what they see. Then, the professor asks them to get up, stand on their desks. From their new perspective the students could see what was actually in front of them; (but behind what was first observed) they saw truly what was there. What was impossible to see from the previous perspective, but what was in fact there the whole time. The professor performs his famous stunt of standing upon the desk to remind the students that we "must constantly look at things in a different way." We need to look from a different perspective. "Just when you think you know something," he tells them a moment later, "you have to look at it in another way."

So, what is the paradigm shift we need to make from the conventional perspective we have and the methods we have used to address our data over the last twenty-five years? The first big shift is to understand that we have, as an industry, partitioned it and siloed it. We must now share it simultaneously and transparently between systems and between departments.

For years we have relegated the data to be lined up in tiny little rows to be counted later and hidden behind an overwhelming array of security features with access protocols that keep us from using it. We have designed the systems to accommodate requests for downloads that are fulfilled by people who get irritated by the idea that they must stop what they are doing and program a special report or perform a data pull. If you work in a company that requires a work order to be completed before you can get to your data for marketing purposes, you know you are trapped in that world. In that world, how could we react in real-time to a customer purchase or interaction and dynamically, instantly, and automatically send the right message to the right person at exactly the right time and in the right place? We can't, and we know we can't.

Conventional thinking and most corporate standard customs based on yesterday's workflows make the process of data access so difficult that most cannot efficiently purpose our data in a proactive, preemptive, and customer-centric way—so it goes unused. We have put people and processes in charge of the data with the mentality of operationally plodding deadlines needed for the completion of payroll, end-of-year budgets, operational planning, monthly billing, and P&L statement generation and asset tracking. These are all long lead time planned cycles where the rewards go to those who are most pragmatic. All of these long lead time and postmortem functions can be perfectly serviced by existing IT and enterprise data systems—that is what they were built to do. The new requirements of dynamic marketing place too much proactive demand on conventional IT systems.

Let's face it, the ingrained mentality of most people working in IT or finance, as well as the processes needed to store data and then purpose that information after the fact, is far different from that in departments such as sales or marketing.

The requirement to use information dynamically to win and keep more customers is not only sales and marketing centric, but can be irritating to existing processes and systems. The simple fact is most enterprise or marketing platforms are designed to accommodate static and latent workflows. There is an organizational paradigm and process change that must go hand-in-hand with the new methodology of one to one dynamic marketing and its superior returns.

I believe one of the reasons we have been successful, thus far, in implementing these new dynamic one to one cross-channel, integrated campaigns in so many different industries and companies is understanding this corporate cultural push back. We have developed a system that does not break into the old world process or mentality with system integration and all that goes with it. If your system—new or old—can write a report, then we can read it and then purpose it for our dynamic marketing needs—all in real-time. No need to start an integration project with the IT team or request stale data downloads that are so difficult to acquire. We all know those static downloads lose their true potential effectiveness by the time we receive and use them.

With the right partner, there is no custom integration required on the client side to retrieve the information that exponentially improves your returns. In addition, on the back side, the results of your marketing activities and client interactions are aggregated in one place—the dynamic dashboard—and then also written back as a report to the client's enterprise, CRM, or other system(s).

We never took anything away, we never had to change the internal corporate process, hardware, or enterprise workflows. We only mirrored the resulting output of enterprise or siloed systems. We then aggregate that output in real-time with our dynamic 1 to 1 workflow and ad serving systems to launch fully dynamic cross-channel 1 to 1 marketing campaigns. Again, if your system can write a report, it can be parsed and used in real-time.

This methodology, process, and technology can be instantly harnessed. We have a turnkey one to one dynamic messaging implementation and strategy process that takes a new customer from start to finish in less than sixty days. The implementation strategy starts with a deep dive audit that, inclusive of audience and brand attribute mapping, content creation and development, database set-up and cross-channel, produces dynamic, 1 to 1 marketing campaign implementation in less than sixty days.

All the enterprise IT team has to do is allow us to embed a piece of code on the server. If you can hang Crystal Reports off your system or any reporting software, the right team can free your data to allow the exponential gains of dialogue marketing on a 1 to 1 basis in real-time, across all your channels in less than sixty days.

As we've seen in this chapter, two powerful market forces are driving the need for micromarketing:

1. Today's individual business and consumer customers are more demanding about getting what *they* want.
2. Communication platforms/channels are changing and multiplying quickly. MySpace went from non-existence to a dominant position over the entire Internet and then, within two years, they were playing second fiddle to Facebook for their existence. The one thing that real-time social networking has provided our economy is a rocket fuel booster to the concept that communications should be and can be "tailored specifically for me" in real-time. Social media have raised the bar for professional marketers to keep up with the fifteen-year-old Facebooker for relevancy in communications.

We, as marketers, can no longer just push our message in front of our customers and prospects; **we must establish a conversation with them, so they *interact* with our marketing communications.** We can no longer just publish to your audiences; smart marketers must establish a dialogue to stay relevant and ensure your highest return for your marketing dollar.

The automated and dynamic segmentation marketing system and resulting new methodology powered by one to one marketing practices allows us to hear what customers are telling us, make sense of that input, and respond to it quickly and profitably. It's a shift away from simply promoting goods or services to offering a better, more personal customer experience. In the next chapter, I'll show you a quick case study of how this system works efficiently to establish true, individual relationships with large numbers of customers—an achievement that simply can't be reached efficiently without this new automated and dynamic marketing technology.

CHAPTER 10—TAKE AWAYS

- The Long Tail strategy provides opportunity for businesses to offer online access to lower demand products as a profitable revenue stream. Find your long tails first.
- Dynamic marketing automation is the integrated system and catalyst by which a successful one to one marketing campaign is delivered. Lead nurturing is the same to dynamic marketing that a tricycle is to a Formula 1 car. Do not be misled by the pieces; you must have them all to complete the puzzle.
- Anticipate and react first and foremost to the behavioral needs of the consumer while providing relevant messaging to your targets.
- Establish a dialogue with customers in each marketing channel by providing personally relevant offers based on previous interactions and touch points built into your marketing funnel.
- Implement and deploy a dynamic one to one marketing campaign by following these linear steps: **strategy + logic + consumer data + content development + distribution.**
- *Share* data in real-time. Do not undertake data *integration* projects; they're a rabbit hole.

CHAPTER 11

Scalability

One to one marketing for everyone

Scenario:

A small business services company uses 1 to 1 cross-channel marketing to increase contacts and sales at an important annual trade show.

Situation:

A small company providing appraisal services to insurance companies and related organizations needed to increase the productivity of their efforts in signing new customer relationships at the industry's largest annual trade show. In previous years, using only ads in the show program and the same size booth space, they had averaged ten sales contacts at the show and converted one or two of those to customers each year for more than a decade.

The activity was a challenging but necessary effort, and in the worst years, when the new customers did not come through from the show, the effort barely paid for the cost of attending the show. This was tolerated because in the good years, they ended up with three new customers and that would make up for the bad years when only one new customer was signed. In addition, this was the only show and point of aggregation for this client's particular niche prospects. The ongoing draw of this show was that it was known as a virtual, "Who's Who" of the industry, and prospects utilized it heavily when considering a move from a current supplier because they could measure the options and make a choice over a weekend. The upcoming show was causing even greater heartburn for the company owner because the industry, overall, was down 20 percent from the previous year and his sales were flat compared to the previous period.

Solution:

An automated, cross-media, cross-channel 1 to 1 marketing campaign.

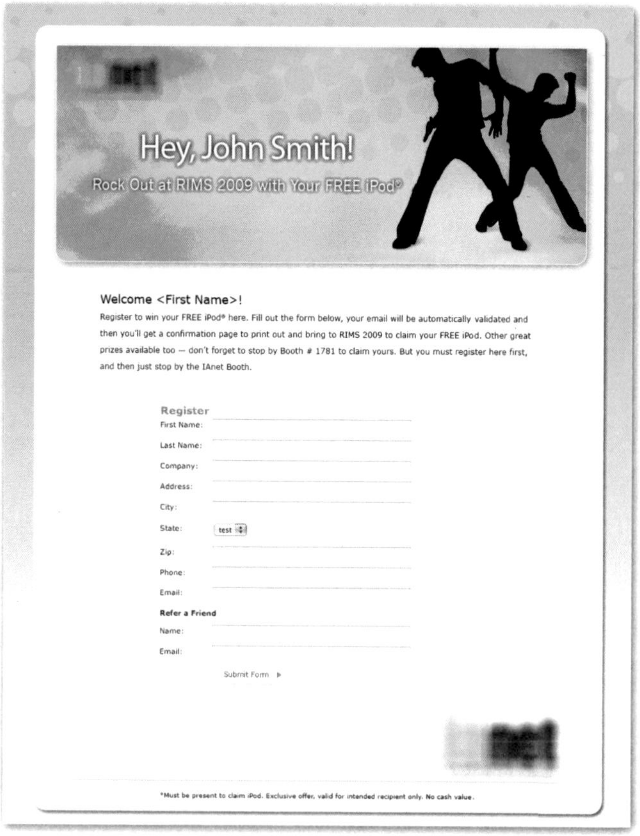

Strategy:

We developed a 1 to 1 marketing campaign with interactive online and offline components, using highly-personalized marketing vehicles. From the total list of prospective attendees, we targeted just over 500 who mapped to our brand attributes among a list of 1800 registered attendees (the one to many list) to be prime prospects for the company. We created direct mail to be sent to each prospect before the show, reminding them to come by the booth or hospitality suite and register for a special gift. The creative was personalized to utilize their actual name and information about their attendance at the show as part of the printed graphics on the card.

In addition, on the direct mail piece, we asked the recipient to go to a link that provided a personalized landing page (a Personal URL, or PURL—for example, www.recipientsname.companyname.com) to register to qualify for a new digital music player. The PURL allowed the prospect to register to win one of five free iPods to be given away at the client's booth at

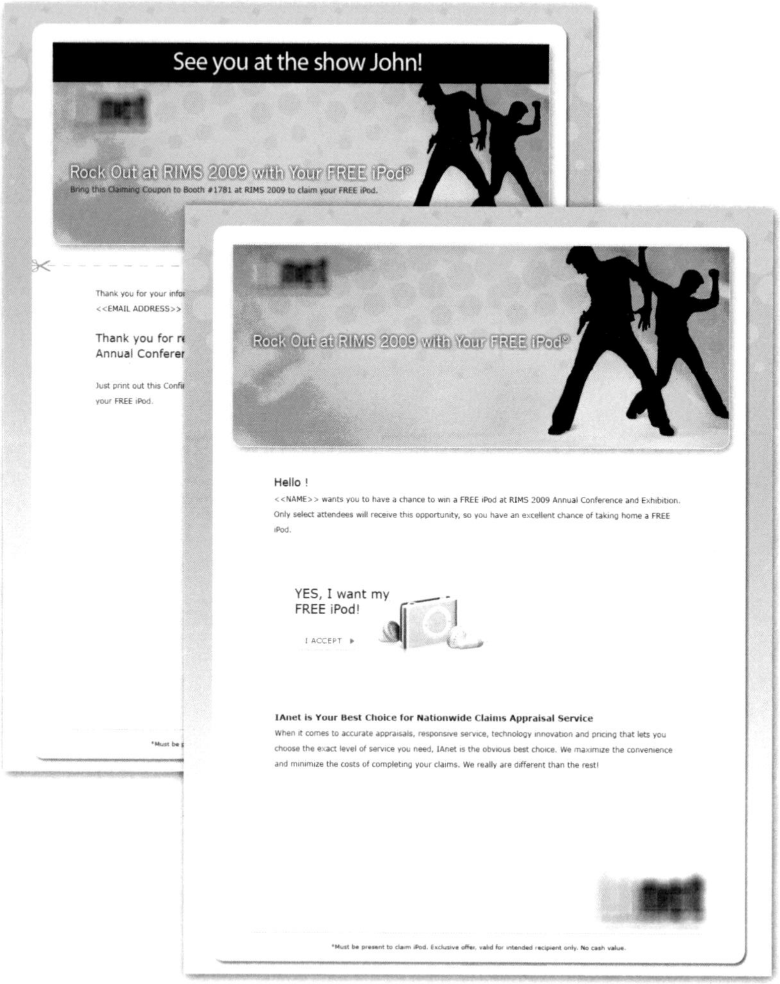

the show. When they registered, they provided their email address and full contact information and the prospects could invite another person attending the show by forwarding the link. The exchange of information allowed us to send email reminders, which also included the hyperlink, to the initial recipients and the referred show attendees about the company, the hospitality suite at the show, and the free iPods. In addition, the information gleaned from this initial touch was databased and dynamically parsed so that it could be aggregated into campaign number two.

Results:

From the total universe of 508 targeted prospects, eight (1.6 percent response) visited their PURL and confirmed their information and attendance at the booth from the direct mail touch before the show. Another nineteen (3.7 percent) responded to their HTML and, ultimately, another thirty-three (2.5 percent) showed up at the tradeshow booth with pre-knowledge of the giveaway from a follow-up call that led them to their PURL. These prospects claimed they did not receive the email or direct mail. They were directed to the registration on their PURL, and these prospects printed their registration prior to attending the show or they kept the direct mail card without registering online and presented it at the booth for the iPod (sixty total responders confirmed and provided a tracked response rate of 11.8 percent). The sixty prospects visited the company's booth at the show as a result of receiving an element of the campaign. Five of the registered prospects who visited the booth were converted to customers within weeks after the show, compared to the average for ten years previous of two conversions per year. This is a 250 percent quantifiable increase in bottom line immediate results. Several other prospects have been converted since the time of the show who attended the show but did not engage at the booth or through the marketing mechanisms. These residual values are also a typical by-product of one to one marketing campaigns. These types of highly personalized dynamic and cross-channel campaigns resonate more than the competitors' based on the professionalism and reach of the campaign. More importantly, 1 to 1 integrated marketing campaigns also pave the way to penetrate corporate firewalls by inducing first contact online by the target, driven from the offline direct mail message. This implementation methodology induced these corporate prospects to type in the client's URL natively, placing the client's URL in the Sent Mail folder and allowing future marketing communications *through their corporate spam filters*.

So, let's look at this small business ROI. For 60 percent more in costs—$10,000 additional costs over the normally invested $15,000 it historically cost the client to attend the show—this client received a 250 percent increase in results (the difference between the average of two sales at the end of a show they had previously enjoyed with their conventional approach versus the five sales the multi-channel campaign achieved). In addition, it is important to consider the quality of the clients was notably higher; they were bigger companies that spent more per company. This is also an attribute of the more professional projection of image. The attending tradeshow salesperson reported, "The new clients we signed with your campaign were more concerned about what we did well than our price." Lastly, the data collected on this first initiative will be utilized in future efforts to refine the messaging and future calls to action.

If you compare the results of this very small business campaign, it becomes typical when comparing conventional one to many marketing costs and results versus the variable messaging of cross-media, one to one marketing campaign methodology deployed for the client. To imagine how this case study may scale up for you, just add zeros to the end of all the numbers reported. This methodology is truly scalable. It is relying on the personal relevance generated with each potential customer and a database of brand attributes that match your targets' hierarchy of needs. As long as those matches can be made, the scalability is linear. The client normally invested approximately $15,000 per year including travel, personnel, and booth costs on attending this show. This included mass marketing mailings inserted in the show attendees' packets and the additional one to many pre-show mailings to the attendees. It is important to note the company's show marketing efforts had previously included the vendors and competitors that would never purchase or influence the purchase of our client's services. With our additional marketing expense and refined methodology, the client invested a total cost of $25,000 to attend the show. The additional $10,000 cost of the one to one multi-channel personalized campaign garnered 250 percent more results for a 60 percent increased investment.

I chose this example to demonstrate that the company did not have to be large. The company did not have to have state-of-the-art resources to deploy this campaign. They did not have to have data systems that shared information across boundaries. They just had to have the foresight to work with the right partner. A firm that has the resources and the experience to generate one to one, cross-media, cross-channel strategies and the ability to map their brand attributes dynamically, to develop the content to be called upon dynamically and the ability to implement that dynamic and personalized messaging cross-channels—where and when the customers chose. We work with multi-billion dollar firms with universes that include millions of customers in sixty-five countries across the world. We also have clients who have very limited dollars to invest annually for marketing. The methodology is scalable across industries, customer segments, and any media channels.

Let's not forget what marketing is all about in the first place—customers want to know, "Is this product or service right for me?" We must keep in mind the customer will choose when and where you will be allowed to present your case. This new methodology allows you to accomodate the shift in the markets at astonishing rates of effectiveness, no matter what the message and to whom.

We have seen how the methodology of Neuromarketology™ is applied to online and direct mail consumers to supplement sales. We have looked at how it is applied in the small business-to-business world in new business development activity.

Now, let's also take a look at how this methodology applies in a larger retail organization driving incremental or additional sales from existing clients. This example is a typical 80/20 revenue growth strategy. Eighty percent of this company's over $1 billion in sales were from 20 percent of its customers.

Scalability Big and Small—One to One Marketing Automation in Action for a Big Business

Scenario:

This example is a clothing retailer with a deeply developed online presence and a goal of increasing its sales from its online division. The goal was to concentrate a strategy on the 20 percent of customers that made up the 80 percent of sales.

Tactics:

A frequent buyer program was developed that targeted multiple buyers by sending a printed invitation and thank you card with an offer of a free personal shopper program if they registered via a PURL printed on an unsolicited personal shopper invitation. The offer noted that the personal shopper program would automatically consider their likes and dislikes and offer recommendations based on their purchases as well as an additional discount on matching purchases. The invitation was sent additionally by HTML with the same information and same PURL call to action.

Once the customer registered via the PURL and offered additional information with the completion of a simple profile, the customer was now eligible for the additional discounts on following purchases. We then mapped each additional purchase with like items based on brand, color, and type of purchase. Upon purchase, a trigger would match the purchase with like matching products. If someone bought, let's say, a pair of shoes, we would offer the pants or handbag that would best match the initial purchase, based on their frequent purchaser profile.

Results:

Purchases within this targeted group increased by 21.2 percent creating an overall sales increase for the year of 8 percent.

Imagine the impact on sales and marketing ROI when thousands of these scenarios play out automatically each day with every one individually timed and dynamically personalized by the system, based on the customer's own activity. It's not hard to see that this real-time, individualized and highly relevant conversation with customers can increase sales as well as customer satisfaction.

Retail Consumer Cross-Sell Micromarketing

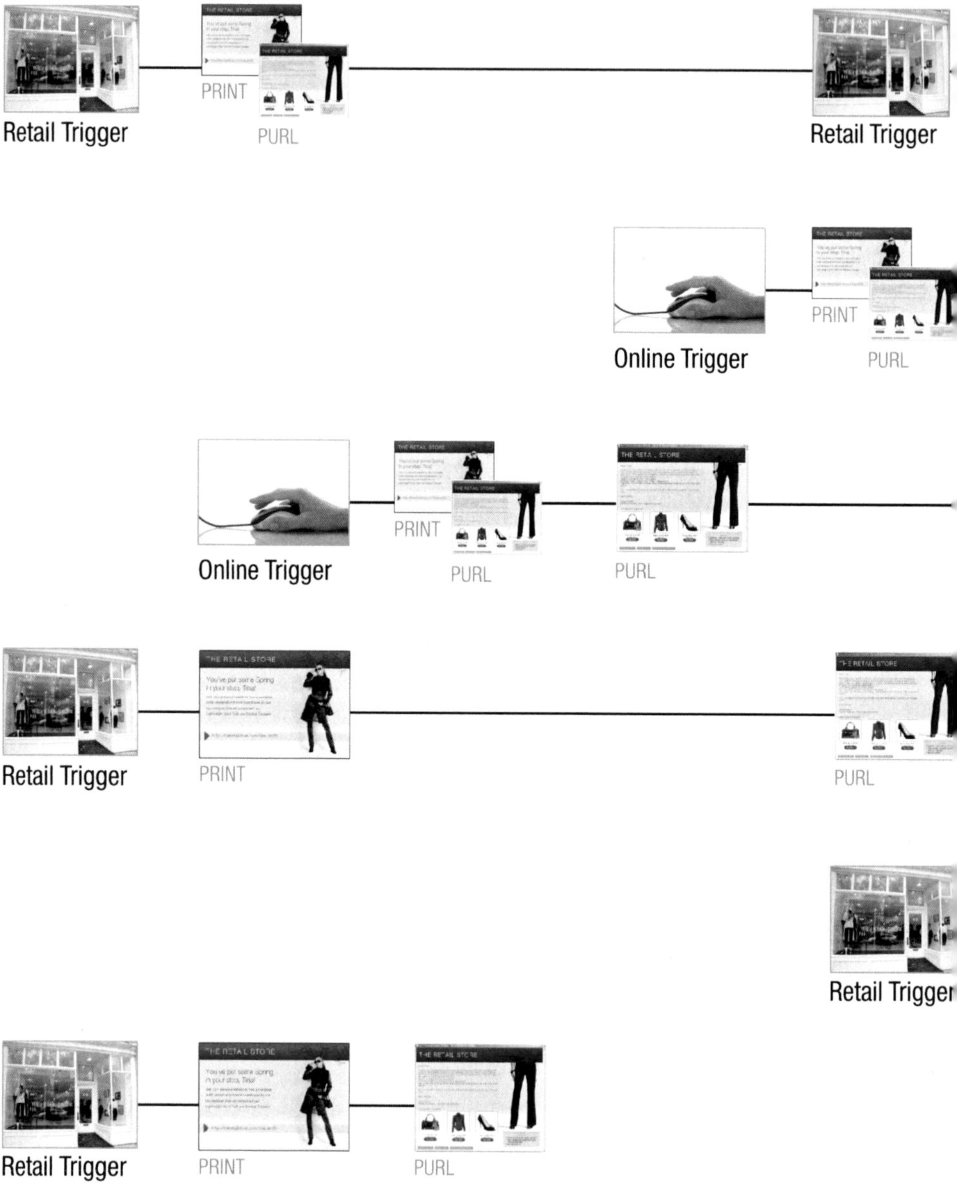

The timing, content, and delivery of each marketing process is driven by the customer's behavior and expressed preferences, individually and dynamically.

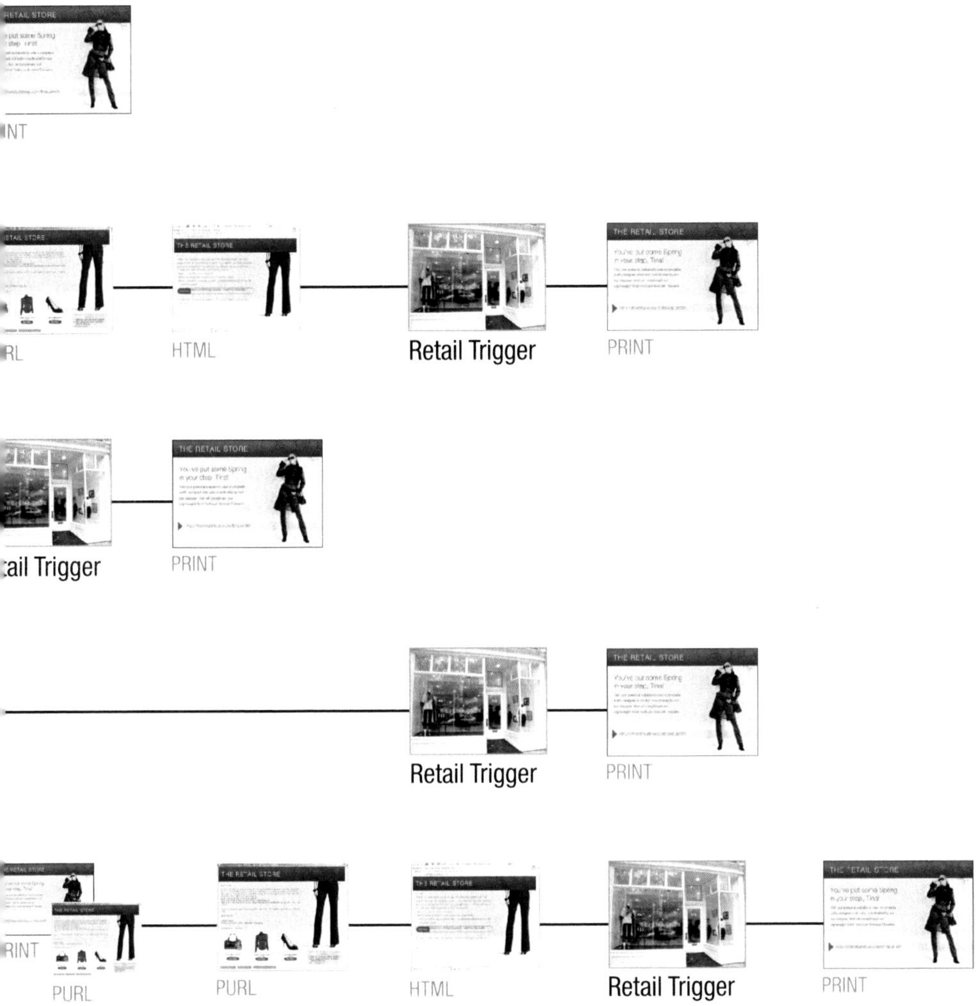
HTML
Retail Trigger
PRINT
PRINT
Retail Trigger
PRINT
PURL
PURL
HTML
Retail Trigger
PRINT

Example of If/Then Dynamic Automated Messaging

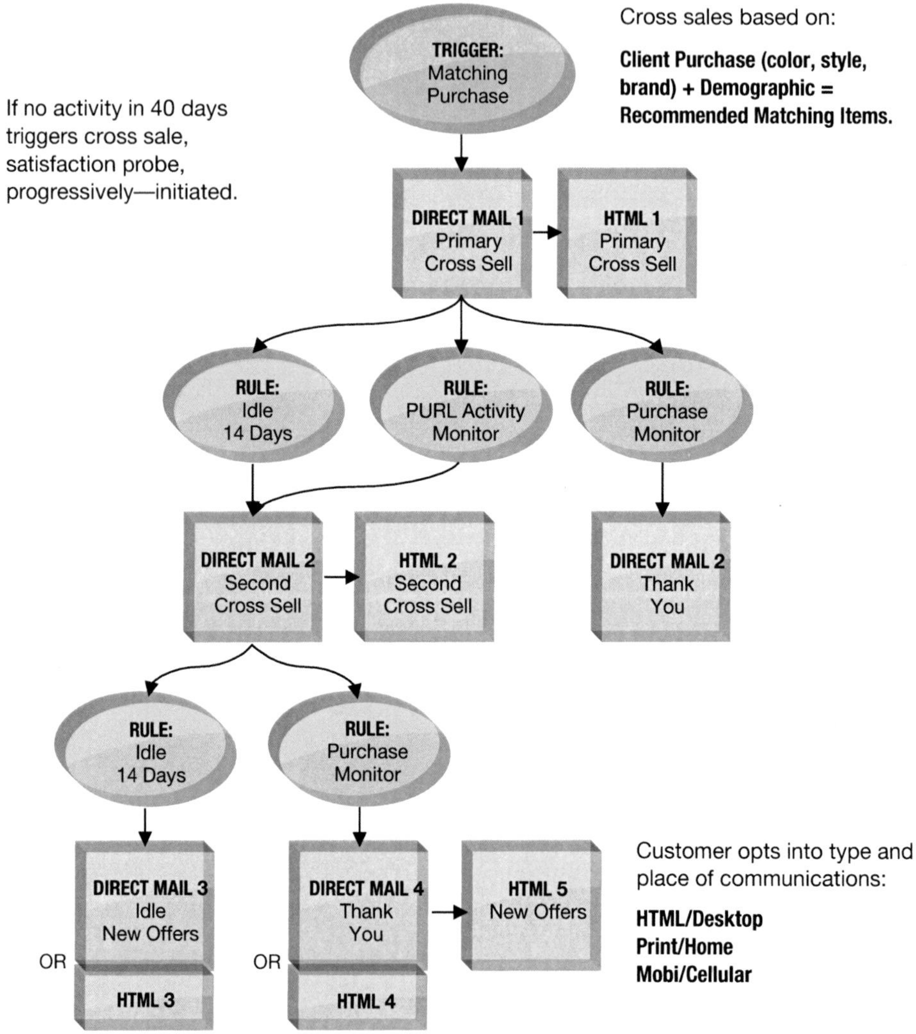
Cross sales based on:
Client Purchase (color, style, brand) + Demographic = Recommended Matching Items.
If no activity in 40 days triggers cross sale, satisfaction probe, progressively—initiated.
TRIGGER: Matching Purchase
DIRECT MAIL 1 Primary Cross Sell
HTML 1 Primary Cross Sell
RULE: Idle 14 Days
RULE: PURL Activity Monitor
RULE: Purchase Monitor
DIRECT MAIL 2 Second Cross Sell
HTML 2 Second Cross Sell
DIRECT MAIL 2 Thank You
RULE: Idle 14 Days
RULE: Purchase Monitor
DIRECT MAIL 3 Idle New Offers
OR
HTML 3
DIRECT MAIL 4 Thank You
OR
HTML 4
HTML 5 New Offers
Customer opts into type and place of communications:
HTML/Desktop
Print/Home
Mobi/Cellular

Retail Consumer

Retail Consumer Cross-Sell Dynamic Workflow

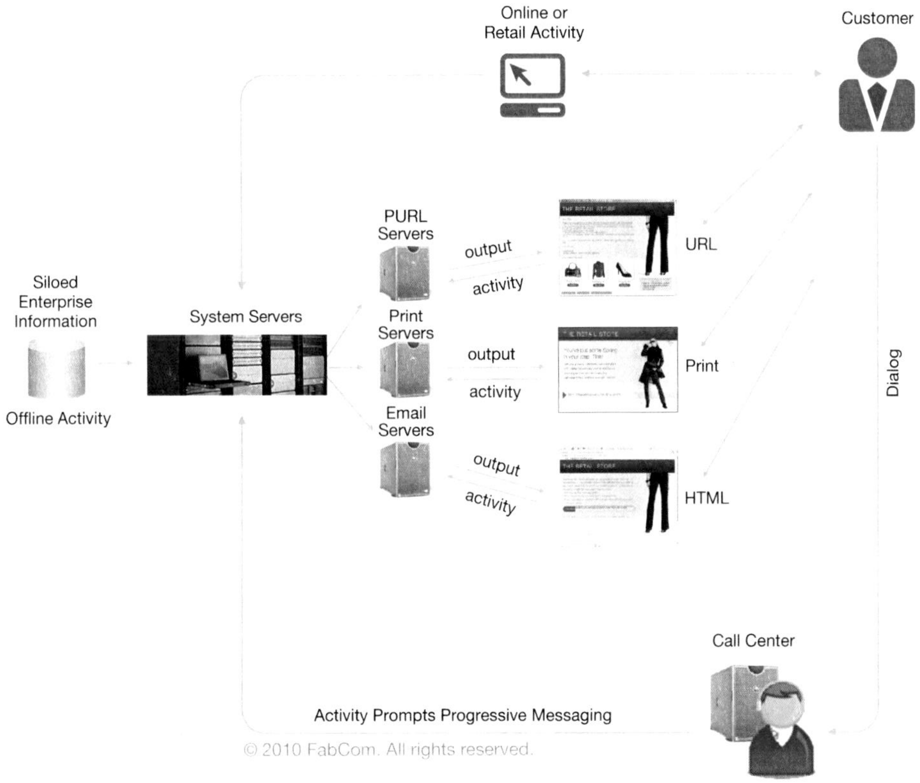

CHAPTER 11—TAKE AWAYS

- The dynamic one to one methodology of Neuromarketing can be applied to any size company and is scalable across all industries, customer segments, and media channels. Find your place in this spectrum and you will know where to look first when transforming your marketing organization.

- A company does not need to have state-of-the-art resources and large data systems to deploy real-time, dynamic one to one marketing campaigns. Smaller companies just need to have the foresight to work with the right partner to help develop and implement.

- When Neuromarketology and dynamic segmentation are applied to larger companies, significant gains in market share can be obtained quickly and at a fraction of the costs of conventional segmentation. This methodology is just another way to accomplish the same results (additional customers or revenue streams into the same organization) as conventional segmentation but at a fraction of the costs and timelines.

- Pick a new launch. Use Neuromarketology and dynamic marketing practices to grow the division. Then after measurement, repeat.

CHAPTER 12

From Mystery to Accountability

Real-time marketing performance metrics

"I think I'm wasting half the money I spend on advertising. But I don't know which half."

- John Wanamaker, Department Store Pioneer

It's my all-time favorite marketing quote. We laugh at it, but it's actually worse than it seems—much worse.

We smile smugly when a baseball player is applauded for being a .300 hitter—successful one-third of the time. But in our business, we are regularly willing to accept 2 percent as a measure of success. While it's possible for a well-planned promotion to make money on a 2 percent response, clearly it's inefficiency with a huge cost. Even with a successful 2 percent return promotion, you have wasted 98 percent of your resources. And it doesn't take a genius to see how ROI can grow exponentially if you could increase the response rate. The shift in paradigms and resulting methodologies and technologies we have discussed in this book make possible the relevancy and timeliness that can increase marketing efficiency with response rates in the double digits. The kind of response rates the big guys get is because the big guys have invested years developing each customer segment. They had the money, the time, and, most importantly, the marketing intelligence to develop their channels with conventional wisdom and conventional methodology.

In order to implement real-time dynamic workflows, we must be able to measure what we are doing in real-time and make adjustments in real-time. I know you just sighed when reading that last line. Most companies are not able to accurately measure the ROI on their marketing initiatives individually, precisely, and quickly by the end of the month and now I am advocating real-time constant measurement of marketing?

What is it about marketing? Every other area of your business provides the accurate metrics you need to manage, plan, make performance improvements, and project future results.

In accounting, you can have a CPA firm audit your books to ensure they accurately reflect your company's business activity. We use those metrics to make better decisions about current operations and future goals. In operations, we account for every single asset and how it was utilized and how that affects the bottom line. We can look at the results of an inventory or fulfillment report for the specific information you need to measure and manage the return on your company's assets.

Where is that hard information for executives to make better marketing decisions and growth plans for the future? Where is the accountability for the results and the return on investment of your marketing? I'm not talking about revenue and disconnected click reports. I'm talking about hard numbers, real-time measurement for *each and every component* of your marketing programs, which allow executives to make timely adjustments in real-time to ensure the ROI of each specific campaign. I am speaking to the idea that "We invested 'this much' in advertising and our return on investment to date is 'exactly this much.'" I'm talking about placing an ad campaign and knowing in real-time what is working and what is not and changing the messaging and tactics before all the dollars invested are lost. We are talking about real-time measurement and subsequent adjustment on the interactivity of each and every element of your marketing campaigns from ad messaging and individual sales results to retail and location-based consumer activity.

Why does marketing always seem a little squishy when you try to pin it down? To begin with, how can you be certain you're putting the right message in front of the right people at the right time? What's the difference in response when you use message A versus message B? Or image A versus image B with copy and call to action C? How do you measure the results? What do you measure? Do you know the ROI of your marketing initiatives—and how to improve it? We, as business leaders, know within a penny the costs versus the ROI in every other area of our company, but not in marketing. I'm talking about having solid metrics, solid insight, and solid actionable information on each marketing vehicle, each advertising tactic, each customer interaction, and each variable within every campaign. No wonder some company leaders feel just like John Wanamaker did.

And, it's not the fault of your marketing team. This lack of accountability has always been the nature of the beast that is *marketing and advertising*. You're dealing with individual human reactions and perceptions. You're dealing with enterprise systems and processes and personnel designed to run the company overall, not the specific unique task of marketing dynamically in a new myriad of diverging channels. The creative process in marketing is not always a straight line. It can be difficult or next to impossible to define fair and accurate measures of return on investment with the timing and feedback of the traditional marketing processes. It's seemingly a professional craft—part art and part (sometimes, not enough) hard science.

In the other areas within modern business, there is a plan and a system; there are relevant, accurate metrics in place. Because of this, you know what's happening and you can use the information to improve performance and focus resources. In marketing, many times we find it's usually anecdotal evidence such as, "Well, no, we didn't actually sell any more widgets with this ad. But we positively impacted our awareness with our prospects." "And," you might ask, "how do you know that and how do I measure the return on investment of *awareness*?" One of my goals in writing this book and crystallizing this type of thinking is to relieve the queasiness of the unknown when it comes to marketing and its transparency.

Automated dynamic segmented marketing and one to one messaging is truly a breakthrough in our capability as marketers to create, distribute, control, and measure the return of marketing and advertising campaigns. It's better, more effective marketing, created with less effort and more resonance with your targets, and tracked in the same finite, precise manner you expect in every other part of your company.

Not only can interactive, online tactics be measured precisely for response and return on investment, so can any traditional media campaign elements, simply by adding an interactive funnel component or dynamic tags, barcodes, and a pen full of offline tactics to connect your offline marketing to your online funnels. This new methodology generates specific, accurate response and real-time result metrics as well as a large volume of other highly qualified data about your prospects and customers. Just as we saw in the case study in the previous chapter, you get not only accurate, target-initiated data, but the system also provides and responds to triggers, constantly moving sales forward and fine-tuning the results and return on investment of your entire marketing operation.

The volume and quality of data provided by the system means, as an agency CEO, I do not have to tap dance around questions from clients about return on investment and what-have-you-done-for-me-lately? This methodology and the embedded tracking that the dynamic application of this methodology provides customers specific, tactical level results, in real-time. At our firm, based on the way we have deployed the methodology, we provide those results right to our customers' desktops—available in real-time through their browser. In addition, as I write this book, we are also testing phone application that our customers can use to tap into their entire annual marketing activity from their iPhones.

Real-Time Response/Activity Metrics on Your Desktop

Because this is an integrated end-to-end workflow system collecting and utilizing data, we are able to see audience responses and activity, analyze it, and present it for review and fine-tuning in straight-forward report formats in real-time. You no longer have to wait and wonder about how to measure the ROI of a campaign or any individual tactic. The audience activity relative to marketing communications is reported right on your computer desktop.

In addition, online and offline tactics can have a broad range of trigger and measurement devices built into them as they are created.

As shown in this illustration, the marketing console that reports results in real-time is part of our integrated dynamic marketing system. The marketing strategy generates individual tactics to reach target audiences through a variety of media points and platforms. Responses to the tactics are recorded in a database, analyzed, reported, fine-tuned as results dictate and the loop begins again.

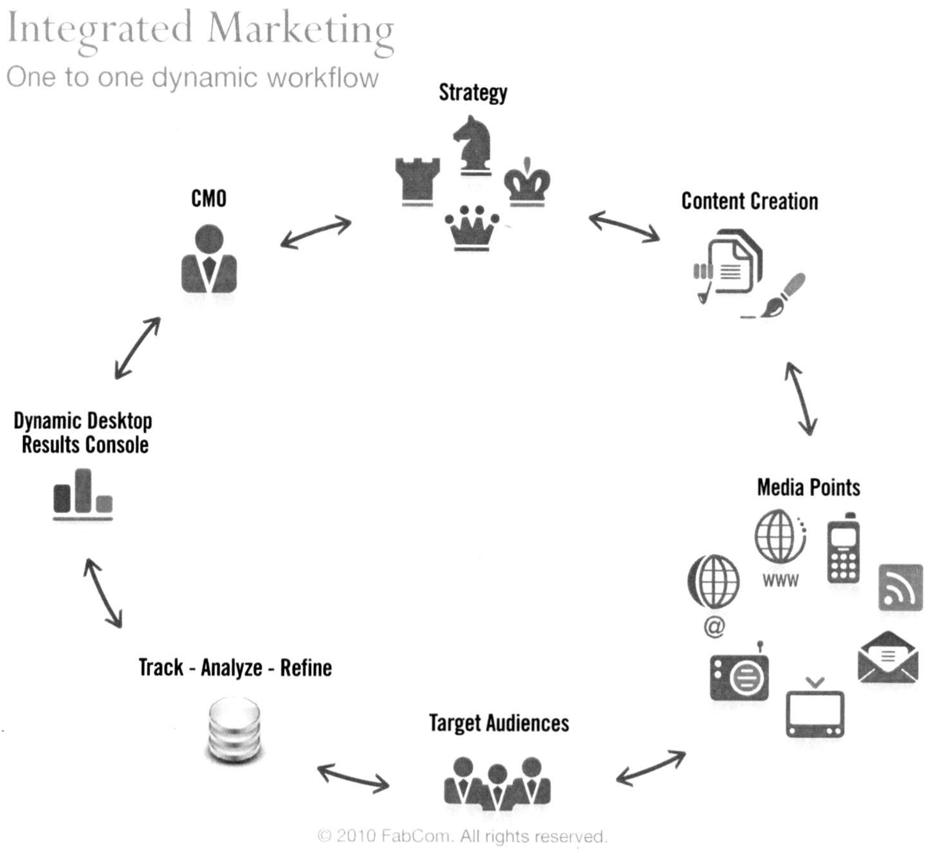

The Marketing Console reports all the data that is available on the integrated segmented marketing server for any and all specific campaigns, as well as data that is tracked by the cross-media interactive elements. This combined data is then analyzed and refined, to be presented in a graphical way to the marketer, by using an Internet browser. The Marketing Console closes the loop for the marketer and adds a large volume of valuable, actionable information for decision makers.

Marketing Console:
Make or Break Business Intelligence in Real-time

These days, marketing is in the moment. There's an ideal time to touch your prospects and customers, and you either hit it or you don't. But with so much siloed activity, analytics, and e-commerce to sort through, by the time you've figured out what's really going on, the moment may well have passed.

Unfortunately, most business intelligence arrives too late to optimize your marketing. Sure it's great to know at the end of the quarter which online initiative hit your benchmarks and which did not. But how much more useful would it have been to know that weeks earlier? Not only because you could have reallocated assets to more effective efforts, but because you could have re-calibrated a given campaign to impact the segments you'd planned on influencing.

To address this essential need of Neuromarketology™ for current, accessible business intelligence, we developed a Marketing Console that gives our clients the data they need to measure efficacy in real-time. Is *it* working?

This is a simple enough question, and the right methodology should enable you to answer it. Not just at the end of the quarter, but at the end of the day. In fact, we went so far as to make our Marketing Console available to our clients as an iPhone app. Because in our new marketing paradigm, business intelligence has to be that available.

ROI Sample Reports

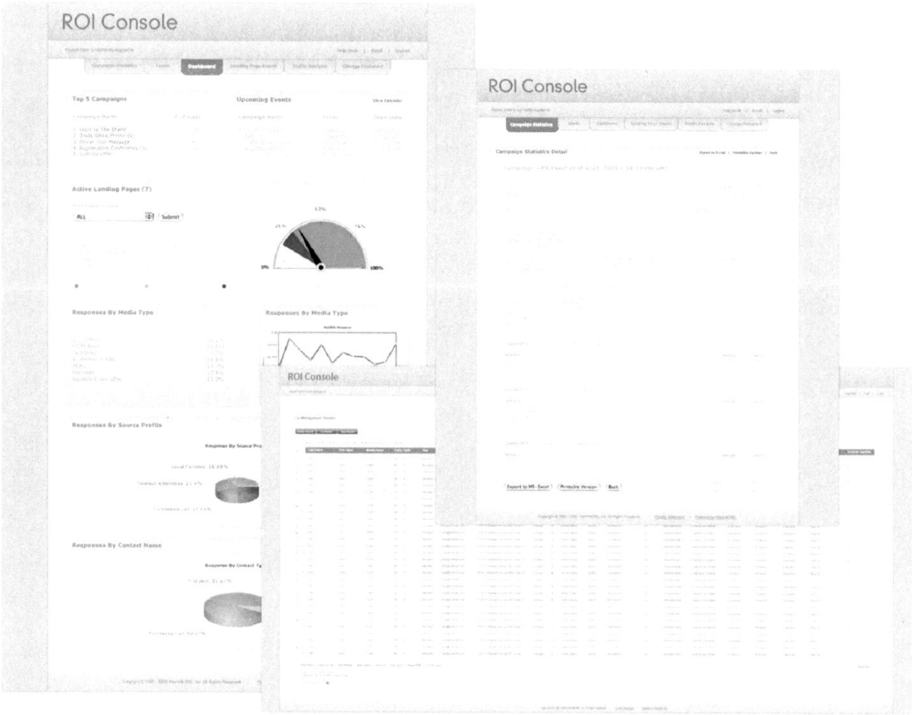

Online real-time dashboard of marketing activities entire analytics.

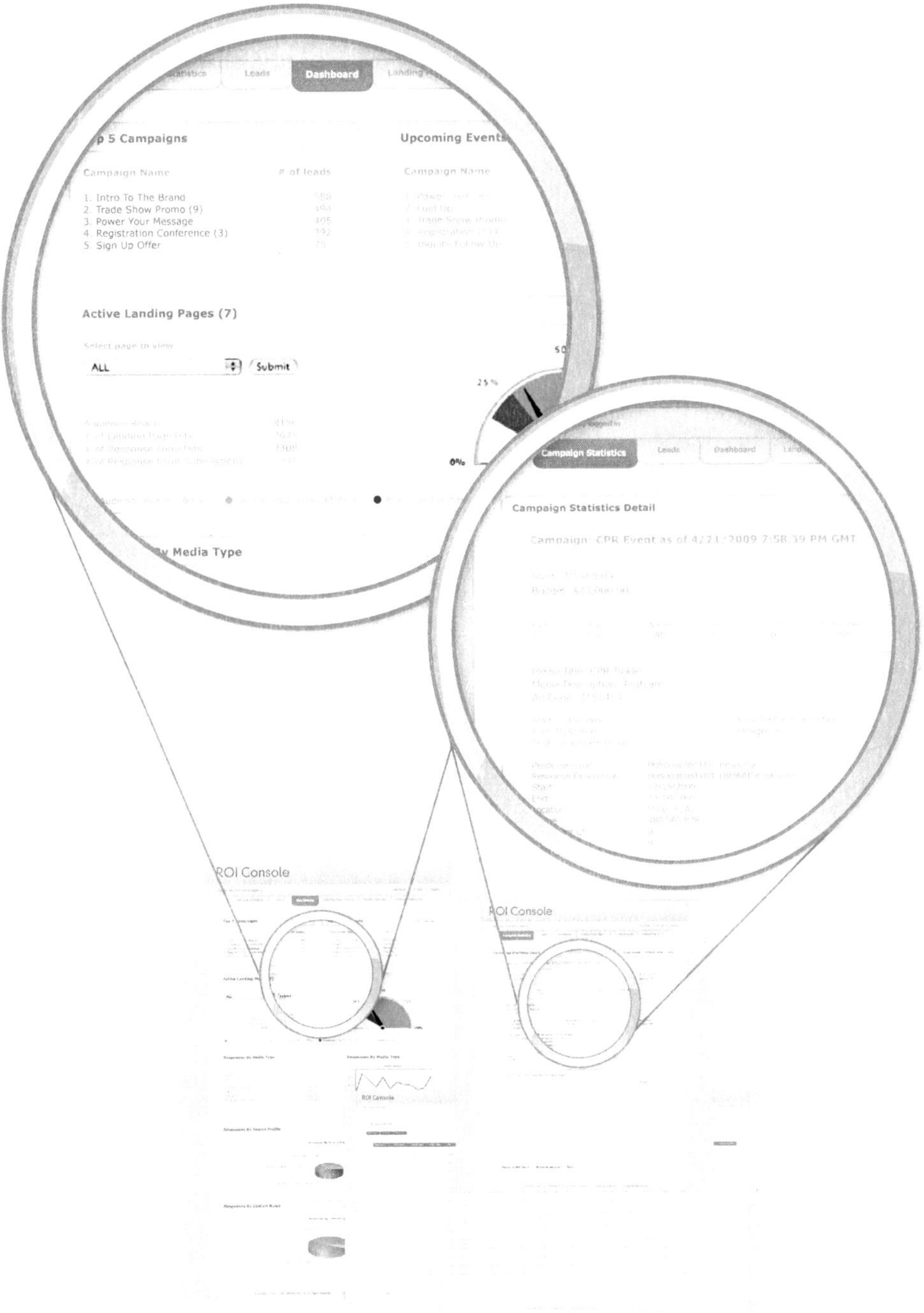
Leads
Dashboard
p 5 Campaigns
Upcoming Events
Campaign Name
# of leads
1. Intro To The Brand
2. Trade Show Promo (9)
3. Power Your Message
4. Registration Conference (3)
5. Sign Up Offer
Campaign Name
Active Landing Pages (7)
ALL
Submit
25%
0%
Media Type
Campaign Statistics
Leads
Dashboard
Campaign Statistics Detail
Campaign: CPR Event as of 4/21/2009 7:58:39 PM GMT
ROI Console
ROI Console

Rapid Campaign Testing/Augmentation

This next diagram illustrates another advantage of the end-to-end dynamic marketing automation system—the ability to quickly test, measure, and fine-tune campaign tactics for best response and ROI. In the case of an online campaign to a group of defined prospects with similar profiles, you can literally send different sets of graphics and messages to three small but statistically valid test audiences at 9:00 a.m. and monitor responses to those. Then, try a fourth version at 2:00 p.m. based on the analysis of responses to the first three, determine which graphics and message combinations and placement options produced the best results, and send that winner out to the full audience after analysis and refinement. This type of rapid-response fine-tuning can also be automated to work in real-time and would be impossible with conventional technology and conventional methodology that tries to connect disparate systems and suppliers and can only do so at great cost or great time delay. This rapid-test capability has a dramatic impact on increasing ROI from marketing tactics and campaigns.

Test Your Campaigns

Give competent professionals three chances to get it right and they will.

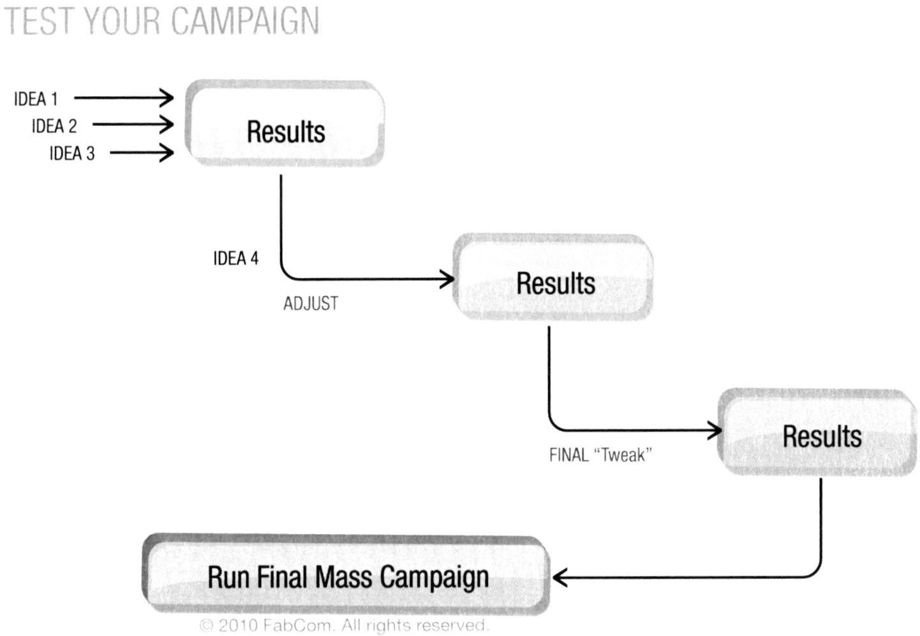

Accurately testing campaign elements becomes an efficient, real-time process. Varying messages and timing can be tested, analyzed, and revised within a 24-hour period to optimize ROI.

CHAPTER 12—TAKE AWAYS

- The greatest by-product of this methodology for in-house marketers is real-time reporting like never before. Drive your organization to have *all* results of each and every component in your marketing mix reported in real time in one place. All online and offline activities including all partners marketing should be available in real-time and online. Drive for it and, just like Google analytics for your webpages, you can have this kind of granular reporting in real-time and with complete automation. Build your marketing to be smart and report to an integrated dashboard. No more dancing for explanations. All the time your team invests aggregating and validating results can now be used to think about how to help acquire and retain more customers.

- Traditionally, metrics were available to measure the efficacy of operating departments within an organization. By utilizing a Marketing Console and dashboard reporting, the results of marketing initiatives are now available in real-time. For the first time, we can measure the efficacy of marketing initiatives, and adjust as they progress.

- Use the rapid-test and real-time message configuration benefits to ensure delivery of the best message, in the best way, to the right audience, in the right place at the right time. Test, tweak, test, tweak, test, tweak, and then fire with rapid informed adjustments.

CHAPTER 13

Your Place or Mine?

The seduction of the status quo

The case for change is an exceedingly compelling one. You've got shrinking returns, increasing risks, a marketing landscape that is obviously radically altered, and a new methodology organically emerging from that landscape that promises not only to meet the challenge, but to exponentially expand marketing opportunities and to do so within reasonable budgets. Why wouldn't your organization jump on this train?

The answer is that the status quo has a way of digging in and holding on. Sometimes, the resistance you face might be institutional, sometimes it's personal. Sometimes it's driven by cynical motivation such as job protection, sometimes by honest confusion, and sometimes by just plain short-sighted stubbornness. In this chapter, I want to help you troubleshoot, in advance, the kind of thinking and attitudes that can all too easily derail this new methodology before it has had a chance to prove itself.

The number one objection is probably that of sheer work volume:

"Are you kidding me? Who's going to do all this? We don't even have enough people or budgets to get this month's work out, much less take this on."

This type of reaction strongly suggests the need for an outside partner with the necessary expertise. Your in-house environment may not be well-suited to designing, developing, and deploying cutting edge methodologies within marketing timelines and existing budgets that conflict with the ingrained perceptions of longtime gatekeepers.

A key strategic decision for every marketer reading this book is:

"How do I deploy? Should I develop the necessary in-house advertising and marketing capabilities or work with an outside agency?"

This one choice can have as much impact on the results of your neuromarketing efforts as any other factor we have discussed. Business is amazing in that no matter how technology-driven we become, success still comes down to sound decision-making. This one decision, for example, could provide the options for your company to run away with early efficient gains. A company does not have to abandon its existing processes and infrastructures to take advantage of the new methodology provided by Neuromarketology™. Companies do not have to be trapped by resources into continuing to do what they always have done until they reach the point of ineffectiveness and depleted resources. The new end-to-end capabilities offered by the thinking driving Neuromarketology™ and dynamic one to one messaging are available to be deployed in sixty days. No software must be purchased, no hardware, no additional staff needs to be hired, and no one needs to be trained, until the returns are proven with outside-in resources and support. This strategy will allow you to take the gains of early adoption. The right partner can teach you how to avoid the inevitable pitfalls of initial implementation.

Organizations with the willingness and wherewithal to develop these capabilities in house are looking at four to eight quarters worth of hard work just to be in a position to launch. Then the real learning curve hits. Our first initiatives were roughly 25 percent effective and 200 percent the cost. It took us two years of inspiration and brainsweat to really start hitting our stride. If you find a content development and implementation company that is truly savvy and competent in this space, they have already invested the years of trial and error. They have deployed the hardware and software. They have seasoned teams executing this type of work daily. They should have teams of researchers as well as seasoned brand and positioning experts to facilitate the mapping of your brand attributes to your targets properly. They should have a hybrid team of programmers that all know a multitude of programming languages and have been trained in a win/win culture that works in perfect synchronicity with the designers, copywriters, and art directors. Then, to top it off, this tightly-knit work group must also have world class IT pros who know how to work with the corporate IT in-house staff to ensure full synchronicity (not integration) with all existing systems.

An option that has worked well for many may be simply to hire the best team you can, that has proven experience in this emerging and converging area, and start reaping the rewards. As you evolve in the new paradigm, use the new knowledge and its superior marketing ROI to help transform your organization. This may be the path of least resistance and most efficient method to harness the power of dynamic real-time messaging and its ability to increase your market share.

The great in-house versus agency argument has been debated for decades. This decision must be continually re-evaluated in light of the changes in the economy, the erosion of mass media results, and the new technology convergence that has led to a hyper connectivity of the markets while, at the same time, they are diverging in their ability and desire to communicate with a brand. Part of the solution for successful marketers is finding new ways to connect to your markets on *their* terms. For small, medium, and large businesses alike, the stakes are higher than ever. The markets are on the move. Getting it wrong could mean not only missing annual benchmarks, but losing major market share to a competitor who acts with maximum intent and follow-through to seize the relevance of their brand over yours with this new methodology. On the other hand, getting it right will increase earnings, while, at the same time, seizing market share away from your competitors.

One way to examine the question is to look at what the big boys do. Remember, these players have deep enough pockets to make their decisions purely on the basis of performance.

A 2008 study by Horsky, Michael, and Silk "The Internalization of Advertising Services," supported by Harvard Business School, found that "the vast majority of large advertisers employ outside agencies." Why do the largest companies—with the highest increases in sales and returning the highest values—outsource their marketing and advertising? Why do these companies demand to work with outside professionals rather than establishing in-house capabilities? These are the companies with the most sophisticated management and information systems (they can measure ROI in a myriad of ways), and they have the budgets to do anything they want. They all have very loyal and intelligent in-house capabilities. So, why do they consistently choose outside, independent agencies for marketing and advertising services rather than staffing in-house capabilities? The reason, from a study by Silk and Berndt ("Scale and Scope Effects on Advertising Agency Costs," *Marketing Science)* quoted in the 2008 paper:

"An in-house agency sacrifices size-related economies realized by an independent agency serving numerous clients. *Use of an outside agency is* *less* *costly than operating an in-house agency.*"

Of course, if the comparison only considers invoiced costs from the outside partner and we compare those exclusively against the hard or incremental direct labor costs, many will proclaim "we saved xyz by doing this in-house." Those that have the ability to measure the total true facility, hardware, software, and lost opportunity costs continue to work with outside partners. An independent agency buys, staffs, and invests for a number of clients. The cost of goods and services is advantageously leveraged, compared to a company buying and expensing only for itself. A great agency has already facilitated hundreds or more projects similar to the one you are about to undertake. A great agency adds value by not only achieving these economies of scale, but by knowing which strategies and tactics can produce the best results for a specific project, whether it's application development, publishing, a media buy, or online campaigns. When it's necessary, a great agency can influence underperforming vendors (based on providing similar work to vendors from ten other clients), so your organization doesn't lose any time to getting the inevitable production or media challenge straightened out.

Not All Partners Are Created Equal

But be cautious of suppliers that talk the talk, but can't walk the walk.

Frankly, at this current time, the majority of agencies, whose sole reason for being is to offer innovative marketing solutions, do not currently possess the know-how or the technology to keep their clients riding the wave. Just as importantly, most do not possess the commitment to every intricate phase from planning through execution, to guide new adopters through the shifting marketing landscape and implant this methodology. As of the writing of this book, there are *fewer* than a handful of companies in the U.S. that have a true understanding of this new methodology and who are currently deploying truly dynamic, end-to-end, multi-channel, cross-channel, integrated one to one marketing campaigns. There are organizations doing dynamic marketing, there are multi-channel campaigns, there are many integrated campaigns, and all of them have a start and a finish. But not many are producing real-time, fully dynamic, cross-media, cross-channel, and fully integrated campaigns and delivering on the full capability and ROI of the new one to one marketing methodology.

The Objectivity Issue

One of the most vital elements in effectively applying this methodology is objectivity. Today's complex, costly, and cluttered marketing environment demands rigor and reality at every turn. As you saw in chapter 5, accurate and insightful audience mapping is essential to reaching ultra-high relevance. To achieve this, we have to be absolutely objective about what our products and services can and cannot offer.

It is normal, and perhaps even natural, for company management and staff to view what they offer the marketplace in subjective terms. A company's employees work hard every day to make their company the best it can be. They are encouraged to look on the bright side, and internal conversations tend to be more enthusiastically received if they focus on the positives. This is well and good from an operations standpoint. But, when it comes to establishing ultra-high relevance with consumers, as we have discussed earlier, you first must have ultra-high objectivity.

Watch out for the tendency among employees and management to be overly-optimistic about a product's strengths and short-sighted about its weaknesses—and every company and every product has its weaknesses. This lack of objectivity can doom a campaign strategy to costly failure. Or worse yet, disguise marketing mediocrity that leaves half the company's growth, opportunities, and profit potential on the table.

The curse of, "but we've always done it this way," weighs heavily on both the strategic planning and creative development of marketing in organizations. This effect is also heightened by the fact that staffs are less likely to say no, even when they know they should, in response to a mediocre or flawed marketing or sales tactic from management.

The right independent agency can help you keep it real, provided a relationship is established where frank communication is welcomed and valued. In this case, an outside agency can bring an external perspective and clear-eyed objectivity to your marketing challenges and opportunities.

Creativity for a New Marketplace

This new marketing methodology requires fresh ideas and a fresh approach to messaging. One way to ensure the status quo wins out, and the new methodology leaves room for the status quo to survive, is to attach bold new messaging initiatives to old, stale marketing creative. It won't work. In fact, more creativity in every area of your marketing communications will be required to achieve the substantial gains possible. Again, this is because we are deploying micromarketing strategies, which means getting personal, visceral, and emotional with people on an on-going basis. So, keep an eye on creativity fatigue. The mapping of your company's brand features, characteristics, and attributes to your target audiences' individual buying criteria requires deep research and thorough strategic thinking. The outcome of a dynamic one to one marketing strategy provides us with what to say, how to say it, and who to say it to as well as when to say it. We then must have the "chops" to actualize and deploy the new insights.

The result of the brand mapping is granular, detailed, and specific, so you can cut through the market clutter and convert your targets. It would be like rowing upstream to try to re-purpose your one to many marketing content on your dynamic, personalized, cross-channel 1 to 1 marketing campaigns. You can't connect to all these new market slices with content recycled from old campaigns that targeted only your traditional 1 to many audiences.

The challenge, then, is to tap into a source of creativity that can keep up with the migration of your markets, including facilitating your ability to reach them consistently and efficiently. Implementing new strategies based on dynamic, one to one marketing methodology will meet your needs and consumers' changing preferences as they emerge.

Owen Butler, former chairman of Procter and Gamble, informed P&G shareholders that the corporation had considered, but ultimately rejected, a proposal to acquire an advertising agency on the grounds that "the creativity of an in-house operation was unlikely to match that of an independent agency."

How important is creative development in the marketing process? Irwin Gross, in his study, "The Creative Aspects of Advertising" (*Sloan Management Review)* examined the allocation of an advertising budget, comparing the costs of creating and developing advertising messages to the outlays for media exposure, and found "advertisers were typically under-spending on creative development relative to media by a wide margin."

True creative minds—the people with the most creative talent—choose passion over pennies. They're not in the marketing game for the money; they want to flex their creative muscles. An influx of new, fresh creative ideas comes from a wide, diverse exposure to others steeped in the advertising culture and business, as well as the experiences of working with varied types of clients, projects, and target audiences.

Human resource studies have shown us a creative will eventually get weary of communicating the same brand consistently, day in and day out. Experience shows us the tendency is eventually trying to personally reinvent the brand just a little bit on each advertising initiative. We have seen this phenomenon quickly dilute brands and marketing communications to ineffectiveness. The double-edged sword is that, if management tries to rein in this sort of brand roaming, the creatives will move on to other companies quickly, exacerbating the "reinvention" dilemma, losing time to training, new staff mistakes, etc. One of the defining positive attributes of working for an independent agency is that the creative and strategic teams get to work on scores of accounts, so they don't get bored and they understand the importance of keeping the brand fundamentals intact.

A great art director needs a great creative director. A great creative director needs a great strategist. They all need a great copywriter. Nothing would ever get done without a production manager to manage all the details. Each member of a cross-capabilities team of advertising professionals needs the other. The interdependence of the team is like that of instruments in an orchestra—each sound blends together with the others to produce flawless music.

The top creative specialists—artists, writers, and now even creative programmers—require the right environment. Outside agencies traditionally offer a more nurturing environment for creative people, making independent agencies superior idea factories when compared to in-house departments.

Or, to put it another way:

> "Organization theory has long emphasized that the type of organization structure that enhances creativity and innovation differs from that designed to facilitate efficiency." (Richard L. Daft, *Organization Theory and Design*, Chapter 7)

> "The fostering of creativity calls for different control and reward systems from those typically relied upon in business organizations." (Teresa M. Amabile, *Creativity in Context*, Westview Press)

> "Concern about an in-house agency's ability to attract and retain creative personnel is often expressed in discussions about the

viability of such operations found in the trade press." (Robert E. Pulver, Association of National Advertisers)

Navigating the Media Madness

Excellent, so you've avoided the pitfall of corporate self-delusion and the trap of creativity fatigue. You've developed a rigorous plan and access to the creative minds you need to execute it. The next mine to avoid in the minefield—mistakes with media and cross-channel implementation.

As we discussed in chapter 2, just a few years ago you could build your whole marketing plan around one or two media choices from the four or five available, and have at least some assurance that you would reach your target audience. A few TV spots, a couple of ads, a direct mail piece or two and, presto, you had the target audience well covered.

Today, not only are broadcast and print media much more fragmented and complex to analyze and buy, but it seems like the next great new media advertising vehicle is being launched on a monthly basis. Where you used to have a handful of decisions to make about media, you may be looking at scores of media channels today, some with hundreds of sub-decisions, in order to reach your target audiences in a meaningful way.

As Bob Liodice noted in, "Essentials for Integrated Marketing" in *Advertising Age*, "Advertisers are faced with the challenge of coordinating a vast array of independent communication services and suppliers."

These days, you need a complete media staff at your disposal with dedicated specialists across the full range of choices available—including emerging media opportunities. It would be a critical error to rely on a media team with limited experience in the full range of channels out there, and then compromise your strategy based on those limited resources.

Media targeting is a significant part of every marketing budget. Only a solid team of professionals with the right experience and expertise can analyze the choices and then buy the correct ones most economically.

Media consumption, in general, is shifting rapidly, driven by constantly evolving new technologies. In times only recently past, it was enough to simply differentiate your marketing communications based on the target audiences' ages. Familiar categories such as "Seniors" and "Boomers" served marketers well in terms of knowing the when, what, how, and why of communicating persuasively with each broad segment. But, just as the media market has gotten more complex and difficult to keep up with, so has the segmentation of target audiences.

Remember, it's about delivering the right message to the right people at the right time and in the right manner. Don't settle for less than a fully capable media team who knows how to speak to your particular customers and prospects, and how they are likely to respond, before you ever begin to draft messages or positioning to influence them. It seems like mind reading, but there is a wealth of hard science and hard-earned marketing experience behind getting this right.

It takes a perfect recipe of demographics, psychographics, behavioral and environmental understanding to complete the strategic brand mapping and reach the target audiences most effectively. All of the areas of understanding are deep with nuances that require a seasoned team of professionals to achieve success. The expense saved by excluding this kind of expertise will be far exceeded by the cost of missing the mark.

Focus, Focus, Focus

Effectively deploying Neuromarketology™ requires a tireless focus on the customer that borders on obsession. So, be certain to keep your eye on the ball, no matter what input is coming at you.

Companies have to meet sales goals, and thus, they can easily lose their way in communicating with target audiences. Sales and marketing are two separate processes. The sales function benefits the company; marketing benefits the customer. The objective of marketing is to create conditions so favorable with prospects that no one needs to sell; the prospect just needs help completing the purchase.

Watch out for the temptation of staff to miss opportunities for customers and prospects because they are too involved with meeting the needs of the day-to-day requests of the sales department, as well as using their resources to accommodate management and operations. In time, if the sales/operational support is not separated from the marketing function, the sales/operations focus will slowly eat away at the lead process. This scenario dilutes the marketing budget and draws resources and energy away from the primary job of marketing: connecting with *new* and existing customers and driving desire for the product/service.

Beware of distractions a company's marketing director/manager may invest four to five hours per day in meetings and preparation for meetings, in order to manage, review, and approve marketing strategies, tactics, materials, and deadlines at the departmental level. Much of the staff also invests a similar amount of time in just trying to administer the marketing programs. In addition, there are the innumerable interruptions from departments other than marketing and sales that need services such as art or copy for operations or administrative functions.

In the Horsky, Michael, and Silk study cited previously, the researchers noted, "Failure to execute advertising to attract consumers promptly can undermine its competitive impact." To ensure maximum effectiveness, your marketing needs to deliver the right message to the right people *at the right time*.

The primary complaint we hear from in-house department users is the lack of a sense of urgency. Be certain to create the dynamics in which urgency is built-in to the marketing process. This is best achieved by aligning your organization with inside stakeholders and outside partners that are serious about accountability.

Good systems are built to accomplish this precisely and repetitively without getting mired down in the politics and diverging needs that are a part of any organization. Previous in-house agency users are often very surprised when a project that might have taken their in-house group a month or more to complete is taken from concept to final delivery in just days.

The agency should help lead the marketing planning and implementation process. The client marketing director/manager should be available for regularly-scheduled marketing meetings to approve decisions and materials and provide direction and needs to be met for the following week at each department level. This leaves more time to truly manage company affairs at the consumer, departmental, and product levels more effectively.

Technology Trade-offs

Corporate marketing departments are often forced to make do with legacy, enterprise-wide information systems put in place by an IT department that serves all the company's information needs across all the different business units. These systems are seldom what the marketing department needs to be *most* effective and efficient in their customer and prospect communications, which leaves them uncompetitive in the market—beaten every time by the outside partners with better technological capabilities.

It's not just that the in-house team doesn't have access to today's latest marketing technology. In many cases they might not even have the latest version of fundamental software tools for creative development and message dissemination.

Without the right technology, the concepts outlined in this book are just that—concepts. It takes the right tools to achieve dynamic marketing, and a compromise in the arena of technology will likely prove fatal to that effort. You need access to the right software and hardware capabilities to make your marketing more effective, more efficient, and—at last—finally accountable.

In-house systems must be monetized, maintained, and amortized over a minimum five-year term (some we see in use after a decade or more) in order to justify a return on investment. This means for the first year after investing, the company is ahead of the technology curve, for the second year it's even with the curve, and from the third year on, it's behind the curve. Three (or more years) out of every five years—at best—the in-house marketing department is behind the technology curve and losing opportunity. For three out of every five years, outside agencies have a huge competitive advantage by this one factor alone—being independent of the delusion factors that drive enterprise level technology investments. Most enterprise, application-specific systems are amortized over five years at best and expensed to a single user.

Lastly, the responsiveness required by the nature of dynamic marketing is not currently supported by most managing business units within *dynamic* marketing timelines. As we have already discussed, IT and procurement march to a different drummer than sales and marketing types. As a result of this conundrum, opportunities can be lost.

The solution? Seek an outside partner with a core business expertise in facilitating these new workflows and thinking processes. You will find business systems, software, and personnel are optimized for a single mission—your marketing success.

People are the Answer

It's a cliché, but it's also absolutely true. The wrong people will bungle the right strategy every time. Be alert not to settle for individuals that happen to be available who do not truly measure up to the task at hand. Being an early adopter and innovator in this emerging area, we have a first-hand understanding of this, knowing exactly what it has taken us to assemble a team that can consistently produce industry leading results. It's not for the faint of heart.

Typically, for a monthly retainer similar to what you would have to pay a single experienced staff marketing professional as an employee, the right partner can *provide a team* of experienced specialists in the various disciplines you will need to perform the myriad of tasks necessary for the creation and implementation of successful dynamic 1 to 1 marketing campaigns. This is a significant benefit from the customer's perspective—you can have as much or as little of a mix of talents and experiences in the myriad of marketing-centric disciplines that are required for effective marketing. The significance is added capacity, experience, and additional talent as you need the services, when you need the output. Clients can turn off the expense or turn up the activity monthly, without hiring, firing, or re-training new employees.

Many CEOs are surprised that when they hire an experienced staff professional to help take marketing functions in-house, that professional must then turn around and hire a number of outsourced individual specialists needed to implement comprehensive, integrated cross-media campaigns.

Below is the roster of a BASE marketing team of professional talent to run a properly staffed team to implement fully dynamic and automated cross-channel one to one marketing campaigns.

Minimum Dynamic Marketing Team

Creative Director

Senior Account Executive

Advertising Supervisor

Account Coordinator

Graphic Designer

Art Director

Creative Copywriter

Technical Copywriter

Marketing Data Architect

Cyber Coder

DB Coder

Web Services Specialist

Media Buyer

Public Relations Strategist

Production Manager

Corporate Strategist

It's important to consider the positions noted in the minimum dynamic marketing team roster are *a BASE team*—a minimum thin band of talent and experience to properly launch integrated, results-oriented, dynamic marketing. A good, independent partner should have seasoned capacity in addition to the base positions at each of the critical talent areas. On average, the staffing levels of an independent agency are three times the base team outlined above.

Another consideration, with the in-house or out-of-house discussion, is an in-house team is often limited to one or a few project priorities at a time, per position, due to staffing levels. If expectations from the business become "we need it *all* on time and *all* working as planned," the in-house employees start reacting to being overworked or underappreciated or underpaid and soon give up on being innovative on each and every project as a matter of survival.

Those of us that are charged with harnessing sales and marketing opportunity know all too well the best opportunities are seized based on having the capacity to accomplish multiple high priority goals simultaneously. A well-staffed independent agency has multiple positions and resources, enough to deliver simultaneous priorities within the same hour, if those are the requirements.

It is their core business. Their entire business model is set to have the capacity to achieve or exceed all of the client's priorities or, as an independent agency understands, next time the client will simply go somewhere else.

The team also brings their previous experience in solving similar challenges many times for other clients. Having done it before for other clients, a great agency has studied the options, avoids the mistakes, and knows what will actually work among the broad array of marketing strategies and tactics.

An outside-in team can also bring successful experience from their similar engagements in industries other than yours and apply them to your challenges. Because of the diversity of experience and background, creative and strategic thinking is not dominated by the perceptions of any one demographic group. Importantly, the right agency is willing to engage in constructive outside-in analysis and frank discussion of the issues that impact marketing success—or the lack thereof.

When hiring a good outside marketing firm, no one has to endure subpar performance until it eventually becomes the norm. An independent agency is focused solely on achieving the priorities and, therefore, ensuring the client is satisfied. The bar of performance and accountability for marketing deliverables is raised to a level of creating interactions where stakeholders *want* to do it again with the same team.

Next, we must consider the operational costs that are also exponential when compared to operational overhead allocations utilized throughout all other areas of the company. A decision has to be made.

Do you create a specialized creative environment to nurture and attract the most creative individuals? Do you treat that one department differently from accounting, IT, and operations? If you do, you have a potential disconnect in other areas of the organization. If you do not, then you will eventually settle for second-tier creative and strategic talent and decisions.

This whole "in or out" discussion doesn't have to be mutually exclusive. Many times clients and agencies find that the most effective and efficient partnerships allocate some marketing responsibilities to internal staff and some to an outside agency. A good agency knows how and where to be flexible so that this shared responsibility works best for their clients. When your internal team and an outside, independent agency work in synergy—each doing what they are best qualified to do—that's often the best of both worlds.

Typically, a company working with an outside independent agency assigns administrative, day-to-day tactical and budgetary oversight to its in-house department. The outside agency would carry the lion's share of the responsibility for strategy (V.P. level coordination helping to shape and drive discussion with key internal stakeholders), creative development, media planning and buying, and production/traffic. Perhaps the company already has a solid public relations person in-house who has good contacts in the trade media. In that case and similar situations, take advantage of the existing expertise and keep that function in-house, coordinating with the outside agency. With a well-crafted version of this type of collegial arrangement, each group stays in its sweet spot for efficiency and effectiveness, while the company reaps the benefits of additional ROI and lower costs.

In the next chapter we'll look at how today's leading-edge technology and methodologies are developing and where they may take us in the future.

CHAPTER 13—TAKE AWAYS

- Be honest and candid with yourself and your company about why you have not already unlocked the power of dynamic real-time marketing. Consider all issues such as human resources and budgets.

- Yes, it's more work initially to produce dynamic marketing. The ongoing returns far outweigh the initial costs. A little more effort produces a lot more R.O.I.

- Seasoned one to one dynamic marketing strategists and implementers are available. They are experienced and can produce a roadmap through the pitfalls of adopting new work flows while simultaneously producing results quickly no matter what your internal systems can handle.

- One to one dynamic messaging is achieved when we brand map your product or service attributes directly to your individual targets based on psychographics, demographics, sociographics, and behavioral graphics.

- Do not simply repurpose your old one to many campaigns into the dynamic channels—they will only produce the same results you get now—utilize a dynamic real-time message construction and distribution methodology and your returns will be exponential.

- Within your company, discuss the idea of data being a real-time asset to your marketing and the differences between a spreadsheet download of stale data and dynamic real-time data.

- It takes a team of programmers, database specialists, strategists, creatives, and media experts all on the same page to implement real-time dynamic marketing. Get your team lined up with the vision before you start.

CHAPTER 14

Connecting the Last Dot

Automated dynamic personalized marketing now

To understand where we are, and how fast we are moving, we need to know where we have been.

Long before Apple debuted the original APPLE, which spurred the desktop revolution, Wang was offering word processing (non-linear typesetting). The innovation was not connected to a cohesive graphical interface nor was it compatible with page layout applications natively. Therefore, desktop publishing was considered and rejected as not fitting the needs of the publishers at the time. The technology was relegated to the label of *fancy typewriter* and was set aside as an outtake, a detour in the long journey toward office workplace efficiency.

The progression of the technology proceeded, but when the final dots were connected to generate the desktop revolution, established companies and industry leaders still declared that it was not yet ready for prime time. This pessimistic assessment was based on their knowledge and experiences *before* the last dot was connected; that is, before the final breakthroughs that yielded the real efficiencies that would transform the industry. They hadn't experienced the newest iteration, so they were still bound by previous experience, even though the technology had moved on. Sound familiar?

In the early days of desktop publishing, I was an evangelist for adopting *that* workflow and the gains it provided our clients. While introducing desktop publishing in the Southwest region, I felt the sting of many arrows fired my way. The established big guys in the industry discredited my message, mostly, I now understand, because of their enormous investments in the old ways and old infrastructure. By criticizing us as early adopters, they were able to buy time in the mind of the market until they could shift their organizations to acceptance, investment, training, and efficiency.

It happened again in the '90s with the early days of the World Wide Web. At that time, we developed strategic plan after plan debuting online strategies for our clients. We faced constant resistance from prospective clients who based their opinions on conventional thinking and conventional experiences. We would recommend laying claim to the online space, building websites, grabbing key words and URLs, putting business processes online and opening up an online store, to name a few. Inevitably, we would be told "my customers do not use the web."

We would show them hard research; we would show them the mushroom cloud of general market acceptance and proliferation. We would show them charts and graphs of their specific customers' profiles illustrating that they had indeed moved to acceptance of the Internet. We would demonstrate case study after case study, just as I have done in this book, on the power of early adoption. In the end, if the potential customer we were talking to did not have experience with leveraging the World Wide Web to connect their brand to the public *and* only had conventional funnels, their status quo paradigms would get reinforced because the only customers they continued to accumulate were also customers who were late adopters. They would then put together customer surveys of their *existing* customers and turn around and say "see, our customers do not use the Internet."

Fortunately, we were very successful with the clients who trusted us and did not protect their old ways, old suppliers, and old experiences based on conventional wisdoms created before the innovation in question was ever available. We grew many multi-million dollar brands for those customers. Some did it just because of the trust we had built with them and were rewarded handsomely. Others did it because they caught the vision and could imagine what could be accomplished if they pursued an online strategy. These customers understood that a progressive thirty-person agency in Scottsdale, Arizona, might just be ahead of the innovation curve and that there *was* a tipping point and that our firm could help them capitalize on it.

This same phenomenon is happening again as I move from industry to industry introducing and implementing these new dynamic 1 to 1 marketing approaches. Today, creating a dialog with your customer based on matching your brand attributes with the customers' wants and needs, and then communicating with them on their terms in the place of their choosing, is the new holy grail of marketing.

It is what great salespeople do on a one to one basis. They understand exactly the difference between each person they are speaking with, and they understand their brand attributes and product features and benefits. They simply adjust the delivery of matched qualities within the offer and the type of customer they are speaking with based on the expressed desires of the particular person they are engaging. This technology revolution allows us to create this kind of hyper-relevancy now on a mass basis with absolute consistency and scalability. Once we do the deep dive and map your brand attributes into dynamically generated customer segmentations, you can be assured you are delivering exactly the right message in exactly the right place in exactly the right timing for each prospect or customer.

The efficiency and power of the technology convergence over the last couple of years in the areas of database, software development, bandwidth, personal output devices, wireless connectivity, analytics, and real-time server reactivity to a customer's interactions with a brand has created a tidal wave of capability that cannot be avoided or ignored.

Many technologies from multiple industry sectors have converged to create a synergy in the most classic sense of the word. Marketers are already utilizing pieces and parts of the new capability, but the true power and return on investment comes from linking these functions together to enable your brand to resonate in a dialog with your customers and prospects. This is instead of publishing propaganda within the deluge of one to many messages that customers routinely ignore, never even getting to or considering the core branding question—"is this right for me?"

The brand mapping of Neuromarketology™ and deploying an integrated 1 to 1 marketing workflow will be as accepted as desktop publishing and the advent of the WWW were. This is a fast-moving train. If you don't get on board now, you'll be left in the dust by competitors who seize the market gains of meeting your customers where they are, on their terms.

Fifty Percent More Earns You 200 Percent in Marketing ROI

I hope I've helped you appreciate both the complexity of marketing today and the significant effort that is required to maximize the opportunity. It is easy to kid yourself with "we're already doing that," but if you are not driving 200 percent more results out of each marketing dollar versus what you accomplished a couple of years ago, then you are not tapping into the synergistic power that makes this a revolutionary approach with exceptional results. If you are not investing the extra 50 percent and getting a 200 percent increase in response, it means you have deployed a piece or two only, or you have not powered your initiative with an accurate strategy, or you have not linked your resources to drive out all the connectivity that really creates the one to one messaging accuracy and added marketing ROI.

It is an easy equation: invest 50 percent more in the initial investment of mapping messaging and creative to *all* the facets of your brand, open up the revenue channels, and receive 200 percent more income, customers, response, sign-ups, whatever goal you're after. When your brand starts to dialogue with relevancy, versus shouting one message from the rooftop, then you will begin to congregate your segments and expand your revenue.

We see marketer after marketer, agency after agency, delude themselves and their companies with pieces of the puzzle that never deliver on the unprecedented opportunity of the whole. I don't want you to make that error. Having read this book, you know there is a unique methodology in deploying Neuromarketology™ in your marketing—especially if you are a small to mid-level business owner or manager with marketing responsibilities. My intention isn't to discourage you.

On the contrary, I want to assure you that the return is more than worth the effort.

Today, any size business can take advantage of the competitive benefits of Neuromarketology™. Even a small business, unlikely to have the resources to fully implement the breakthrough methodology and technology, can reap the benefits by engaging the few firms like ours that have the resources in place to effectively deploy the concepts of Neuromarketology™.

For large businesses, assembling the required methodology, technology, and expertise may make excellent strategic and financial sense in the long run. Proceed with your eyes wide open. It takes different kinds of strategy, it takes different kinds of creative, it takes different kinds of copywriting. And, it cannot be accomplished via an IT department designed to service the core business as defined in conventional terms. Neuromarketology™ requires an IT workflow and IT workforce that operates on marketing time with the attitudes and urgency of marketing teams. That's a whole different rhythm and pace than the rate at which IT teams traditionally take on and facilitate projects. If your IT department requires a work order before you can get something done, then do not even try to bring this into your company without guidance from experienced professionals who have already implemented the workflow.

The right strategists, creatives, software, programmers, workflows, and servers are all specialized for the task of dynamic 1 to 1 marketing. For our larger clients, we write the strategy, design the campaign, and then provide templates for expansions in-house. In effect, we teach larger companies how to fish the new way, augmenting the capability of the in-house marketing department.

Neuromarketology™
Dynamic Segmentation

© 2010 FabCom. All rights reserved.

For smaller organizations, this may be highly impractical, if not impossible. But, small businesses can take heart in knowing that we have deployed these powerful campaigns for less than $25,000 for some clients. By understanding the opportunity now available, you can begin to deploy this methodology to your advantage, whether through in-house resources or by partnering with carefully-selected strategic suppliers.

Organizations can now harness the rapidly expanding power of the *Google generation* for growth instead of being overwhelmed by it. You can abandon the old paradigms, conventional wisdom, and legacy technology of one to many marketing and utilize the concepts of Neuromarketology™ to dramatically increase the return on your marketing investment; at the same time, you can multiply your brand's reach by utilizing the myriad variations of connections possible when we effectively cultivate one to one audience pools instead of applying the methodology used in the past. When you deploy the brand mapping of Neuromarketology™, media fragmentation is no longer a threat to your strategy; it's an invaluable ally that you can leverage to deliver improved results more affordably and effectively. That's the power Neuromarketology™ can bring you.

We have deployed these concepts in multiple market spaces in the last couple of years in the business-to-business and business-to-consumer environments, for both traditional and not-for-profit entities, for big businesses and small. We have deployed this new methodology to market a $30 nutritional supplement as well as to increase enrollment for a prestigious private university. It has worked for delivery companies, resort properties, retail, credit unions, and insurance companies. Customers just want to know one thing when making a purchase, and it's the same thing for every purchase: *"Is this product or service right for me?"* When you answer that question with superior relevance, timing, and placement, sales soar.

The Opportunity within the Chaos

The technology today and all the new media channels can make marketing extremely challenging for many businesses. But when you've got the right systems working for you, it's really an incredible opportunity for growing your business.

The key to success with the technology and methodology of Neuromarketology™ is full implementation. It's possible to see efficient savings when simply deploying content aggregation initiatives with legacy technology. You may also achieve the benefits of content control. But the real exponential returns come when everything is linked to an end-to-end dynamic electronic publishing workflow. The content aggregation initiatives implemented by in-house marketing departments years ago were just the tip of the iceberg; something many times more powerful emerges when content aggregation is linked with the newest technologies in marketing.

Unless you've got deep, deep pockets—or a leading edge marketing partner—the strain on budgets and resources to effectively implement a dynamic segmentation strategy under conventional thinking and circumstances will inevitably force you right back into the same old bad habits.

Conventional wisdom says you can't hit all the markets, so you've got to prioritize. Where do you get your best ROI? *That's* where you put your money. Whichever segment or segments you choose, inevitably you now know you will consciously disregard large numbers of people who map directly to some of your brand attributes. Conventional wisdom demands the proverbial sacrifice of the many for the one. Bottom line: the idea of singularity in customer targeting and messaging has been good and has worked for decades. But now that our markets are migrating away from mass media, clearly we must readjust as marketers. One to many marketing or mass messaging was designed to work in the mass market channels. If your customers are no longer all huddled around the Cosby show with the unified voice of Mom and Dad and grandparents dictating opinions, then you might want to rethink your approach, your partners, and your baseline of beliefs. If Neuromarketology™ and 1 to 1 messaging is implemented from the existing legacy technology platforms, costs, and timelines to develop new divisions, the hiring of product managers, separate sales forces, and separate marketing campaigns will drive your costs through the roof. This type of conventional channel development can only provide the needed return on investment for those with the cash and years to see it through.

Remember, **marketing is no longer about publishing to your customer—it is now all about creating a dialog with your customer.**

Does this mean that the brilliant work of Trout and Ries no longer applies? No, it applies more than ever, only in a distributed approach. These principles of branding and positioning continue to anchor successful, efficient marketing, which can be driven to previously unattainable heights of sales and accountability if the old tenets of messaging are adhered to but delivered on a true 1 to 1 basis.

So Where is This All Going? And How Fast?

While no one can truly predict the future, the one thing that has proven true is that one of the immediate results of technological innovation is more technological innovations. The pace of technological breakthroughs fuels itself, growing ever faster.

What might the future look like? Consider that two-year-olds today are amusing themselves with electronic devices on which they can draw characters and modify them via a touch screen, in which different types of swipes and scratches produce specific on-screen responses. How fluent do you think these little ones will be with technology when they reach their twenties? Will they even think of drawing as something limited to pen and paper? Probably not. It's much more likely that their definition of drawing will automatically include interactive technology.

If you think today's teens and twenty-somethings are permanently tethered to their electronic devices, just wait until this toddler's generation gets to high school.

I think it was Joe DiMaggio that said, "Making predictions is extremely difficult, especially about the future."

Predicting the future can be dangerous, particularly when the role of new technology is underestimated. Ken Olson, founder of Digital Equipment Corporation, one of the pioneering American computer companies, told a trade conference audience in 1977: "There is no reason for any individual to have a computer in their home." Western Union responded to Edison's invention of the telephone this way, "This telephone has too many shortcomings to be seriously considered as a means of communication. The device is inherently of no value to us."

When it comes to marketing, there is no outer limit on where technology will take us. Remember Tom Cruise walking around in a shopping district in the futuristic thriller, *Minority Report*, being bombarded by highly personalized holographic ads meant specifically for him? It's already starting to be a reality. NEC has developed smart kiosks with special advertising screens and a camera that takes pictures of consumers who stroll past. The kiosk uses biometric recognition routines to determine the age and gender of the consumer in the photo and then presents content on the screen that is relevant to the recognized personal profile.

The techy buzz phrase for this sort of thing is "context-aware pervasive systems." The system is everywhere and it knows what you're doing and who you're with. Also known as "ubiquitous computing," it means your target audiences are going to be accessible anywhere and you will know all about them. Some are already worried about loss of privacy, but because the consumers' perceptions drive the marketing relationship, those marketers who use the new technology to present customers and prospects with personally relevant marketing messaging will succeed.

How could this play out in the not too distant future? Let's say you're visiting relatives in a town you've never been in before. You're strolling down Main Street. In the distance, you can just make out the sign for a coffee shop that's part of the chain that also includes the one you've patronized before in your hometown. All of a sudden your cell phone beeps. You check it and find you've just received a coupon for $1 off a cappuccino at the coffee shop you're approaching—in a town you've never been in before. New technology and "geo-fencing" have just presented you with a little gift from the future. The context-aware pervasive system knows you're in the neighborhood, and it knows you like that brand of coffee shop. This takes "the right message to the right person at the right time in the right place" to a whole new level.

Another twist on the same scenario: you're walking down the street when you hear someone speaking to you, but there's no one else around. The mystery voice speaking to you says, "You know those Nike running shoes you've been looking at? There's a Runner's Roost store on the next block, we have your size, size 13s, in stock in red and blue, and if you purchase them today, we'll knock $15 off the price. Come on in." Technology well into development today can locate and identify you by your cell phone and then broadcast an audio message that is so specifically focused to your location that no one but you can hear it.

How about dynamically generated aromas triggered via RFID and exact GPS location of the shopper and resourced by last week's purchases as someone is approaching the bread section in a store? It's not as far away as you might think. The leaders and innovators are working on it right now. As futuristic as the current state of marketing that I have described may sound, it is really only the beginning. Can you imagine the power of sending individually personal and contextually relevant marketing messages to specific people in shopping centers, on the street, or while they're online considering an investment? iTunes' "Genius" recommendations and Amazon's "Just For You" suggestions are examples today. In other words, getting their attention while you know they are considering a purchase in your product category—does the phrase "Holy Grail" ring a bell? We are there right now.

And let's not forget about the inexorable march of recommendation engines or software code that gives us advice about what a buyer may want to consider next. Neuromarketology™ was the early influencer in this phenomenon that has quietly penetrated corporate America over the last ten years. Seven years ago, after seeing the first Amazon engine, we were creating dynamic recommendation engines as an alternative to direct visitors within our clients' websites to the most appropriate messaging without having to create an entirely new website presence for each audience. We utilized the breakthrough as a tactic to provide target segmentation without the costs of a complete website rebuild.

Over the last decade, recommendation engines have become ubiquitous with the Google generations buying process. They seamlessly appear like bird songs in our ear with sites like Amazon, Netflix, Genius from Apple, YouTube, TiVo. Forrester Research says one-third of customers who notice recommendations while buying on a website actually buy something based on the recommendations generated by the software programming.

Think about what is driving those applications. It is the same kind of if/then programming we have illuminated in this book. We break down human behavior into data sets, then look for the patterns that match up. The software's recommendations can become incredibly relevant and fiendishly accurate. The methodology inside a recommendation engine is attempting to second guess the mystical and seemingly completely erratic behavior of the human mind.

And what is the most erratic and unpredictable output of the human mind? Think about the decisions and emotions triggered by the human mind as related to romance. How about the emotions encompassing the mission of finding our one true love or the selection of a spouse or romantic partner? What could be more unpredictable, mystified, and relegated to the never-going-to-figure-it-out pile?

Ever heard of Match.com or eHarmony? Think about the progressions in predictive algorithms we have made, over the last decade by those of us that have been toiling with the subcomponent parts of this technological evolution. The leaders in the industry have been applying them to commerce where and when we could to drive intermediate return on investment.

Now with dynamic databases and proliferation of communication devices we have a massive convergence of capability. When we string together the capability, the outcome allows us to tap into the key information that buyers unconsciously radiate about themselves and their personal preferences all day long in a plethora of interactions within a myriad of communications platforms. We now have the ability to capture that info and then purpose the data in real-time to help reshape the reality of your prospects in real-time. It provides an endless feedback loop between you and your customers.

Why does this become necessary? The new long tail economy has created a deluge of choice in an area people cannot usually get enough of—CHOICE.

The book, *The Art of Choosing*, by Sheena Iyengar, informed us that in 1994 we had five hundred thousand consumer goods for sale in the U.S. Now Amazon offers twenty-four million all by itself. We must provide our lizard brains a path to make the choice.

We have all been glossed over by the rows and rows of thumbnails when searching for a product. Now think about all the other choices we are inundated with. One to one dynamic marketing methodology offers you, as a smart marketer, a solution that allows your company to cut through the clutter and resonate over your competitors' choices.

These are just a few examples of the sorts of amazing tactics that will be deployed, thanks to the methodologies and technologies that we have discussed in this book. We stand today at the very beginning of a game-changing evolution of marketing. So, let's carpe diem and harness those market share gains; start playing now, before the action passes you by.

CHAPTER 14—TAKE AWAYS

- Remember, marketing is no longer about publishing to your customer—it is now all about creating a dialog with your customer.
- As leaders, our responsibility is to continually understand the incremental changes in technology that can provide an advantage for your company.
- Be aware that most great business breakthroughs are the result of many seemingly inconsequential and disconnected evolutions of existing practices that someone purposed innovatively.
- You must invest more to get more. Invest more time mapping your brand attributes to your segments holistically, comprehensively, and emotionally. Invest more in building the systems to automatically

generate your messaging and invest more time thinking personally about your customers. For that extra work, you will return 200 percent more out of your ongoing monthly advertising spend.

- Implementing dynamic marketing campaigns is similar to a mathematical equation. One missed step will substantially change your end result. Each step in the methodology empowers the next step exponentially.

- This is only the beginning of a long march to more and more personalized and dynamic marketing. As this arena develops, it will dominate all communications. You now have the opportunity to be an early practitioner of a new ruling marketing methodology.

- The convergence we are experiencing is bringing us all together again as it gradually segments out the individual. Our mothers, our children, and our peers are all part of the same generation for the first time in history—the "Google Generation."

- Smaller companies can buy the dynamic marketing bandwidth from full service providers effectively without investment in internal systems. If the campaign is orchestrated properly, the additional costs of initially hiring a qualified dynamic marketing partner will be recovered by the results of the campaign.

- Larger companies can test, develop, build expertise, and gain market share by partnering with organizations who have already invested years in the learning curve and can provide the benefits of early adoption without the risks and pressure on existing systems.

CHAPTER 15

Pep Talk Time

Yes, you can!

So, we come to the end of our in-depth look at the future of successful dynamic one to one marketing in the new online, socially connected, and technologically dispersed twenty-first century. It is my true wish that I have helped you achieve an understanding of this very complex subject that, as marketers, we cannot afford to ignore. The tipping point we are approaching mirrors the desktop publishing revolution in the mid-'80s and the Internet adoption of the early '90s. All of the pieces I have illustrated have been around and utilized in some form or format before the publishing of this book. But, they have not been joined together in an integrated approach, with strategy founded on the new capability of messaging, and coupled with a specific methodology of mapping your brand attributes directly to each of your potential customer groups (See illustration on page 151).

When all of this happens together, when all of the evolutions are synchronized, they create a revolutionary way to reach your audiences no matter where they are, and usher them across the chain of marketing progression from awareness, to consideration, to purchase, to loyalty at phenomenal rates that provide unprecedented ROI.

Resources for Our Readers

The baseline of this book's subject matter will continue to evolve at an accelerating rate. Therefore, we are publishing a URL at the end of this chapter to a site that will provide updates as well as larger graphics than could be included within the 6" x 9" format of the book. We will also provide new and additional illustrations to help you communicate the concepts within your organization. As the marketing industry continues to reinvent itself, updated information will fill in the inevitable gaps in knowledge and direction between the time this book is first published in 2010 and the date this book is read. In addition, we are launching www.the1to1.org in 2010 to meet the growing need for emerging information for users and implementation teams of dynamic cross-channel one to one marketing.

There are many organizations and information sources solely powered by the manufacturers of the software components or hardware components of this methodology. They have one objective—to place their equipment and software with you before a competitor does. This supplier agenda may not always mesh seamlessly with your own need for unbiased, application-based information provided transparently. As a result, it can be challenging to acquire the kind of detail needed up front to accurately set corporate expectations, much less complete an honest resource requirements assessment.

A quick word about software/DB and hardware solutions and the providers.

One solution does not fit most applications of this methodology. Each company, in each and every industry, has a different marketing funnel. The internal SWOTs and marketing processes are unique. And this equation is also compounded by the difference in customer segmentations and targeting. One solution will perform admirably in its primarily designed function. We have seen customers who were sold Baha 1000 cars to run an INDY race and wonder why they are losing. Our firm has woven together the best of three different platforms to enable our team to efficiently complete each different tactic in our marketing funnels. We have many clients who use all three and then some. I cannot imagine what would be sacrificed, or lost advantages justified, if we had not created the end-to-end system with so much elasticity, or had to settle on one supplier's set of solutions.

The critical question you undoubtedly would want answered is "will this investment do this *and* that?" It's a question that may not always be answered with your best interests in mind. Just stand back for a minute and think about it objectively. Sales and technical reps are trying to sell something. You then are asking them about an additional buying criterion. If they do not answer positively, the deal could be lost to the next supplier who *can* do that task efficiently. In over two decades of investing in new technology and doing my part to push the industry forward in the Southwest, I have yet to hear one rep say, "We can do it, but it will take you tons of extra investment in other hardware and software and unproductive workflows and many times longer than using my competitor's services."

The processes and methodology in this book will be impossible to implement if the wrong investment is made in initial resources. On the other hand, if all of the pieces are aligned and working together, you will receive superior returns, and the appreciation of an organization that is embracing change for bottom line benefit.

I would like to remind marketers of the analogy discussed earlier in the book of pulling off the road to find a CD in your trunk just to change the album you are playing. If changing the CD is such a hassle, then you simply will not change the music. You will turn it off or seek another alternative.

When it comes time for you to implement these processes and you start getting resistance in your organization, remember, they are all thinking about having to stop and get out of the car just to change the CD. So you may well need to remind them that there is a way to do all this while cruising down the road to superior returns.

But this is dependent on implementing the new methodology as a whole, rather than cherry picking the parts that seem easiest to deploy.

Implementing incompletely, with some of the old practices and some of the new, is like converting your new car to steam power to save gas. It is expensive, it is ugly, and it will not serve your needs. But a true implementation is like shifting from analog to digital. Suddenly, the options multiply, the opportunities clarify, the clouds part, and the very elements of marketing today that threatened your bottom line, now boost it to unmatched levels.

This is the end of the book, but the beginning of the journey. No doubt, as you progress into this brave new methodology, you will encounter new insights and challenges you may want to share. I welcome emails from any readers who have questions, comments, or need guidance about investing in the thinking and practice of Neuromarketology™ and the future of dynamic cross-channel integrated and personalized one to one marketing.

CHAPTER 15—TAKE AWAYS

- You can do this. It's logical, linear, and provides exponential results for those that deploy integrated, automated, dynamic, personalized, one to one marketing.
- Be careful when making software and hardware investments. All software and hardware are not created equally. Half of the game is imbedded capability; the other half is after-sale support. The biggest and most expensive suppliers are not always the best. Ask the right questions and then listen for integrity in the responses.
- Remember, the rewards go to the brave, diligent, and focused.

WHERE TO FIND OUT MORE

Book correspondence can be sent directly to me at:

brian@neuromarketology.com

Need More? Check out these links for additional information:

Updated charts and graphs
www.Neuromarketology.com

The most recent information and user
group and peer advice network
www.the1to1.org

Our full service integrated marketing agency
www.fabcomlive.com

Our agency blog
www.fabcomblog.com

Our data company
www.databasesegmentation.com

Our online project based company
www.scottsdaleinteractive.com

BIBLIOGRAPHY

Anderson, Chris: *The Long Tail*. New York, NY: Hyperion, 2008

Bond, Jonathan and Kirshenbaum, Richard: *Under the Radar*. New York, NY: Wiley, 1997

Covey, Stephen R.: *7 Habits of Highly Effective People*. Glencoe, IL: Free Press, 2004

Covey, Stephen R.: *Principal Centered Leadership*. Glencoe, IL: Free Press, 1992

Du Plessis, Eric: *The Advertised Mind*. Philadelphia, PA: Millward Brown, 2005

Gladwell, Malcom: *Blink: The Power of the Tipping Point*. New York, NY: Little, Brown and Company (Time Warner Book Group), 2005

Kurzweil, Ray: *The Singularity is Near: When Humans Transcend Biology*. New York, NY: Viking Adult, 2005

Lindstrom, Martin: *Buyology: Truth and Lies about Why We Buy*. New York, NY: Doubleday, 2008

Renvoisé, Patrick and Morin, Christophe: *Neuromarketing: Understanding the "Buy Buttons" in Your Customer's Brain*. Nashville, TN: Thomas Nelson, 2007

Ries, Al and Trout, Jack: *22 Immutable Laws of Marketing*. New York, NY: HarperBusiness, 1994

Ries, Al and Trout, Jack: *Positioning: The Battle for Your Mind*. New York, NY: Warner, 1987

Tzu, Sun: *The Art of War*. Birmingham, AL: Cliff Road Books, Inc., 2008

GLOSSARY

Automated Dynamic Personalized Marketing

The ability to automatically create and distribute individual versions of a marketing initiative, each specifically personalized with custom imagery, calls to action, and messaging to the recipient.

Awareness

The beginning stage of marketing communications' impact—when individuals become aware that the product/service/brand exists and may be a viable choice for them.

Brand

The image of a product or service in the market—the sum total of the promises the brand makes to its target audiences through marketing. It is a symbolic concept created within the minds of people and consists of all the information and expectations associated with a product or service. As marketers, we seek to align the expectations of the brand to create the impression that a product or service brand has certain qualities or facets that define it for others.

Brand Facets

The individual qualities or attributes of your brand (e.g., best quality, wide assortment of options, convenient, etc.), similar to the facets on a diamond. Each facet can be mapped to a corresponding target audience, creating hyper-relevant messaging.

Brand Integrity

A promise that a company makes to customers, prospects, and the market in general. For a brand to have integrity, every experience customers and prospects have with the company should ring true to the brand's promises or marketing messages.

Brand Mapping

The process of connecting each quality or facet of a brand to its corresponding target audience in order to make the most relevant appeal to each prospect and customer, based on their individual perceptions, expectations, and place within the buying cycle. Brand Mapping allows you to honestly communicate your brand coherently in different ways to different people.

Cloud

Cloud is used as a metaphor for the Internet, based on cloud-like illustrations used in the past to represent the telephone network, and later to depict the Internet in computer network diagrams. Cloud computing is Internet-based computing, in which shared resources, software, and information are delivered to users' computers and other devices on-demand.

Content Aggregation

The process of collecting content or marketing assets—Images, copy, and other resources from multiple sources in one real-time accessible place.

Context-Aware Pervasive Systems

Also known as "ubiquitous computing," the best known example of this technology is perhaps the scene in the futuristic thriller, *Minority Report*, in which Tom Cruise walks around a shopping district being bombarded by highly personalized holographic ads meant specifically for him. With advancing technology, we will be able to address individual members of our target audiences directly with highly relevant, personalized messaging, wherever they happen to be.

Convergence

Previously separate technologies such as voice (and telephony features), data (and productivity applications), and video that now share resources and interact with each other synergistically creating new efficiencies.

Cross Channel Marketing

A particular set of marketing messages and assets that are displayed to the targets in more than one channel of media such as online messaging and/or print direct mail and/or TV and/or radio.

Cross Media Marketing

Marketing communications in which the message and/or call to action will invite the recipient to cross-over from one medium to another. For instance, a printed marketing piece which directs a prospect or customer to an online micro-site.

Customer-centric

Describing a company that organizes and operates—marketing, sales, operations, service—with a focus on responding to the needs, perceptions, and behaviors of its customers, rather than internal considerations. Many more companies claim to do this than actually do it.

CRM

Customer Relationship Management—The strategies and tactics utilized by a company for managing and nurturing their interactions with customers and prospects. It involves using technology to organize, automate, and synchronize various business processes through the use of detailed information about the customer. The overall goals are to find, attract, and win new clients, nurture and retain those the company already has, entice former clients back into the fold, and reduce the costs of marketing and client service.

Database Marketing

Marketing tactics implemented utilizing databases of customer and/or prospect information, history, etc. to generate personalized messages to them. The information is typically "siloed" in multiple databases that do not communicate with each other, limiting functionality and benefits. In the new age of Neuromarketology™, leading-edge technology and software allow optimum relational access and coherent use of all data, across silos, in order to create hyper-relevant messaging to each recipient.

Dialog Marketing

Dialogue Marketing

To engage "opt-in" customers and/or prospects in an ongoing dialogue through marketing tactics based on responding to the clients interactions by crafting responding messaging relative to their last interaction or current status. Think of a conversation versus a presentation.

dpi

Dots per Inch—also, pixels per inch; a measurement of the resolution of a graphic file. The higher the number, the better the resolution of the image.

Dynamic

Within the context of the technology discussed in this book, I use the term "dynamic" in a specific sense, meaning the capability to automatically generate and modify content or experience; content that is personalized or actualized for each individual and continually updated automatically to refresh or customize content. The content is retrieved from a database automatically and assembled for personalization online or in print on the fly as needed.

Dynamic Marketing

The ability to automatically revise marketing messaging, placement, and timing of marketing in real-time in order to ensure personal relevance to each individual recipient.

Dynamic Cross-channel Integrated Marketing

Integrated messaging across multiple sales and marketing channels or media, using automatically revised marketing messaging, including placement and timing of marketing in real-time in order to ensure personal relevance to each individual recipient. The application is usually used to drive sales and branding to one channel through the use of another channel.

Dynamic Messaging

The ability to change copy, graphics, offers, etc. in real-time and automatically in order to deliver personalization and hyper-relevance in marketing vehicles for individual recipients, utilizing technology and knowledge of the recipients' current and past preferences, behaviors, purchases, responses, and place within the purchasing cycle.

Dynamic Segmentation

Dynamic segmentation is the task of creating marketing segmentation automatically based on if/then programming that assembles the client's interactions and correlates it with siloed data and uses that information to select what type of messaging that particular prospect should receive.

Entry Portal

Also known as a web portal or links page, it presents a variety of information from several sources in an organized manner. Web portals typically offer a search function and other services such as email, news, stock prices, etc. Examples of public web portals are Google, MSNBC, and Yahoo!

Flighting

Scheduling media insertions over a time period in order to maximize exposure for a given budget.

GURL

A Generalized (or Generic) URL (see definition) is also known as a "landing page." It is a specific website address mentioned on a marketing piece that directs recipients to a page on a website created especially for that campaign. In this use, all recipients of the piece see the same content when they visit the website, as opposed to a PURL (see definition) in which content is personalized for each recipient.

HTML

HyperText Markup Language is the most used markup language for web pages. It provides a means of annotation to structure a web page for text such as headings, paragraphs, lists, and other items.

If/Then Programming

A style or category of programming languages having patterns as data types whose values can be manipulated in all ways permitted to any other data type in the programming language by providing strings of code generated during execution that can be treated as programs and executed.

JPEG

Joint Photographic Experts Group—a common standard for compressing and displaying images electronically.

Lead Generation

Using marketing techniques to find and initially interest prospects in order to gather information that may be used to continue the marketing conversation effectively and relevantly.

Marketing Automation Platform

A dynamic, end-to-end, cross-media, cross-channel, micromarketing integrated system of technology and software that delivers the power of true one to one marketing using stored data to automate production and delivery of hyper-relevant marketing communications to specific recipients.

Marketing Console

A comprehensive desktop analytics tracking and reporting application that can, when implemented with the correct technology, monitor and provide real-time data on the results of any and all, multi-channel marketing initiatives and advertising campaigns. Allows marketers to make marketing decisions and adjustments utilizing 100 percent current results data.

Marketing Resource Management (MRM)

Platform consisting of software, hardware, and processes to harness, measure, and direct your marketing resources.

Microsite

An Internet term referring to an individual web page or pages meant to function as a supplement to a primary website. Typically used to provide additional information or purchase opportunity to move the viewer further along in the sales funnel.

.mobi

A top-level domain in the Domain Name System of the Internet (along with .com, .org, etc.), "mobi" is derived from mobile, indicating its use by mobile devices for accessing Internet resources via the Mobile Web. All .mobi sites must be optimized for viewing on a mobile phone. This means websites may be optimized for the special capabilities and restrictions of mobile devices, such as smaller screens, device form/size, etc.

Multichannel Marketing

Utilizing separate channels to communicate to a designated target audience.

Neuromarketology™

Neuromarketology™ is the study of reactions driven from the core brain based on the exposure to specific marketing messages, imagery, and timing. It's the science of knowing each of your target audience's emotional connection points and methodology of configuring your marketing messages to connect your brand attributes with each stakeholder in the most relevant manner for that specific target.

Neuromarketing

The act of utilizing quantitative studies of the human mind's reaction to marketing messages (Neuromarketology™) to configure marketing messaging to reach your targets with hyper-relevancy. By "brand mapping" your messaging to the individual targets through a detailed methodology based on matching the brand's attributes plus Neuromarketology findings, as well as behavioral, demographic, and psychographic, real-time information gleaned from the targets' own interactions, to create dynamic and unique marketing responses per target in real-time.

NTSC

The National Television System Committee sets standards for analog television systems used in most of North America, South America, Japan, and several other countries. NTSC is also the name of the U.S. standardization body that developed the first broadcast standard in 1941.

One to One Marketing

1 to 1 Marketing

Marketing strategies and tactics that communicate interactively and directly with a specific consumer. Knowledge of current and past preferences, behaviors, purchases, and responses allows for a hyper-relevant conversation that delivers the right message in the right place at the right time.

Operational Recommendation

A recommendation of a tactic or tactics to neutralize one or more restraining forces.

PDA

A mobile device that commonly has a color display and audio capabilities, enabling it to be used as a mobile phone, web browser, or portable media player.

Positioning

The process by which marketers try to create a clear image, identity, or differentiation for their product or service—their market position—in the minds of their target audiences.

Proximity Messaging

Utilizing a mobile device's GPS capability to determine the device's location, then analyze the proximity to a commercial location in order to send a relevant message (news, discount coupon, etc.) about the offerings at the commercial location to the mobile device. For example, you're walking past a McDonald's location and get a message on your smartphone offering you a free drink with any sandwich purchase at that location.

PURL

A Persistent Uniform Resource Locator (PURL) is a URL that does not directly describe the location of the web page or information to be retrieved but instead describes an intermediate (more persistent) location which, when retrieved, redirects to the location of the final resource.

Radio-frequency identification (RFID)

The use of an object (typically referred to as an RFID tag) applied to or incorporated into a product, animal, or person for the purpose of identification and tracking using radio waves.

Real-Time Variable Content

Content displayed dynamically on the fly based on real-time interactions with the company or its messaging, by retrieving actions in real-time to be taken from a database and combined instantaneously with the reactions of the target to achieve a specific and relative message.

Real-Time Personalized Variable Content

Content displayed dynamically on the fly based on real-time interactions with the company or its messaging, by retrieving actions in real-time to be taken from a database and combined instantaneously with the reactions of the target to achieve a specific and personalized message that's becomes incredibly visceral and relative.

Restraining Force

Anything that might hinder a key audience from receiving a company's marketing communications and/or making a purchase.

RFID

Radio Frequency Identification—The use of an object (called an RFID "tag") on or incorporated into a product, animal, or person for the purpose of identification and tracking by a reader, using radio waves.

Some tags can be read from several meters away and beyond the line of sight of the reader.

ROI

Return on Investment

Secondary Influencers

Anyone or anything that has influence on the decisions and behaviors of a member of your target audience.

Segmentation

The study and categorization of target audiences into subgroups of individuals or organizations sharing one or more characteristics, beliefs, or values that cause them to have similar needs and expectations and require a unique communications approach.

Silo

A database system that cannot communicate with other, related database systems. The term is typically used to describe management systems in which the focus is inward and information communication is vertical.

Social Media

Communications created to be disseminated through social interaction, using highly accessible and scalable publishing techniques. Social media use web-based technologies to transform and broadcast messages into social media conversations. Examples are Facebook, MySpace, Twitter, blogs, wikis, etc.

SQL

Structured Query Language—a common computer language used to manage data in a relational database.

SWOT

Acronym for "Strengths, Weaknesses, Opportunities, and Threats," a structured and focused way to analyze a company's environment and marketing possibilities and challenges in four critical dimensions.

Touchpoint

The interface of a product/service/brand with customers, non-customers, employees, and/or other stakeholders—before, during, and after a transaction.

Traditional Media

Print, radio, and TV ads, static direct mail, billboards, etc.

URL

Uniform Resource Locator—geek-speak for website address (e.g., www.neuromarketology.com)

Variable Content

Content displayed dynamically on the fly based on certain criteria, usually by retrieving content stored in a database.

INDEX

C

D

E

K

L

M

N

Y

ABOUT THE AUTHOR

Brian Fabiano is driven by a passion to find a better way. Immediately prior to establishing Fabiano Communications, he pioneered the development of High Definition publishing processes in the graphic arts industry at the emergence of the digital revolution. On the strength of this innovation, he piloted the explosive growth of a private company and its ultimate sale to a public corporation.

Today he is CEO of Fabiano Communications, an integrated strategic marketing firm and advertising agency. He's also a nationally recognized business visionary and has been called upon by both corporations and trade associations to share his expertise and insight in one to one marketing, dynamic segmentation, positioning, branding, sales, lead optimization, and strategic planning.

A championship AAU and NCAA certified youth basketball coach, Brian understands the power of a team. He excels at creating high performance, collaborative environments both within his companies and in concert with clients. His style has always been distinguished by frank, upfront communication and a commitment to collective success.

In the areas of finance and strategic planning, Brian has an extensive knowledge of organizational development and the intricacies of mergers and acquisitions, as well as product and service introductions. On the operations side, Brian has developed and implemented sales force automation programs, database management platforms, and real-time fulfillment systems for information and hard goods within all major industry sectors.

A significant side note is that Brian deployed one of the first Macintosh publishing systems in the graphic arts business in the Southwest. He was an early computer innovator and in the vanguard of desktop publishing and implementing the new digital workflows of the '80s. He again helped lead the charge in the '90s, developing online brands and teaching traditional brands how to reach new markets utilizing the Internet. Currently, he is leading the industry in its next tipping point, the application of dynamic segmentation and automated personalized one to one marketing.

By integrating powerful, new knowledge about how the human mind responds to marketing with leading-edge media/communications technology, Brian Fabiano and his team developed Neuromarketology™ to deliver hyper-relevant messaging in any marketing channel as well as measurable branding and purchase preference. From insights about the human mind, to more effective branding and positioning, to sophisticated, multi-channel integrated dynamic marketing systems, this twenty-five-year industry veteran is known for his easy-to-understand language and his colorful, "rubber meets the road" perspective.

As a hands-on Dad, Brian supports his two children in their efforts as academic athletes to compete at the highest level of club travel basketball and volleyball. He once traveled back and forth from New York City to Phoenix twice in thirty hours to attend one of his children's national championship competitions.

"Kids and animals always love me," he says, "it's the adults that need convincing."

Brian has earned the reputation for "getting it done," even in the face of long odds. He has a talent for cutting through the BS, mobilizing teams to work together, connecting the dots before others do, and the integrity to implement properly, no matter what the restraining forces might be.

Brian lives in Scottsdale, Arizona, with his wife, son, and daughter. In addition to coaching basketball, he loves the thrills of big mountain skiing and the serenity of sailing. He is also a "classic Italian with the biggest of hearts" who has a passion for supporting underprivileged athletic youth initiatives.